ELEMENTS OF EPISTEMOLOGY

THE MACMILLAN COMPANY
NEW YORK · BOSTON · CHICAGO · DALLAS
ATLANTA · SAN FRANCISCO

MACMILLAN & CO., Limited
LONDON · BOMBAY · CALCUTTA
MELBOURNE

THE MACMILLAN COMPANY
OF CANADA, Limited
TORONTO

ELEMENTS OF EPISTEMOLOGY

BY

JOSEPH THOMAS BARRON, S.T.D.

Of the Faculty of Sacred Sciences of the Catholic University of America

NEW YORK
THE MACMILLAN COMPANY
1931

NIHIL OBSTAT
REV. ARTHUR J. SCANLAN, D.D.
Censor Librorum

IMPRIMATUR
✠ PATRICK CARDINAL HAYES
Archbishop, New York

November 11, 1930.

COPYRIGHT, 1931,
BY THE MACMILLAN COMPANY.

All rights reserved—no part of this book may be reproduced in any form without permission in writing from the publisher.

Set up and electrotyped. Published January, 1931.

SET UP BY BROWN BROTHERS LINOTYPERS
PRINTED IN THE UNITED STATES OF AMERICA
BY THE FERRIS PRINTING COMPANY

TO A. B. B.

A REAL, BUT IDEAL, REALIST

PREFACE

THIS book is an introduction to the scholastic theory of knowledge. It is intended as a textbook for students who are beginning the study of this branch of philosophy. Its elementary character necessitates a selection of the problems of epistemology that are to be treated as well as a simplicity in their discussion. The author, well aware that the process of selectivity and simplification in the exposition and criticism of philosophical systems is a perilous undertaking, has, notwithstanding, aimed at both. The number of authorities cited is a sufficient disclaimer of any originality of doctrine. If there is anything novel in the book it is its manner of presentation. It divagates from the conventional treatment of the epistemological problem as found in scholastic manuals. In extenuation of this departure from the traditional mode of presentation the author submits that his approach to the knowledge-problem seems to him to have certain advantages over the traditional presentation.

The author is deeply indebted to the Right Reverend Monsignor Edward Pace, S.T.D., Ph.D., of the Catholic University of America, for the counsel he so generously tendered during the preparation of this work. He also acknowledges his gratitude to the Reverend Leo. L. McVay, M.A., who read the work in manuscript.

J. T. B.

CONTENTS

		PAGE
PREFACE		vii

CHAPTER

I.	EPISTEMOLOGY, ITS NATURE, DEFINITION, IMPORTANCE AND HISTORY	1
II.	THE INITIAL ATTITUDE TOWARD KNOWLEDGE. THE METHOD AND DATA OF EPISTEMOLOGY	14
III.	THE NATURE OF JUDGMENT. SKEPTICISM	27
IV.	AUTHORITY, INNATISM, INTUITIONISM	36
V.	PRAGMATISM	44
VI.	SENSATIONALISM	52
VII.	RATIONALISM, PURE AND CRITICAL	70
VIII.	MODERATE REALISM	86
IX.	THE TRUTH OF KNOWLEDGE. REALISM	98
X.	SUBJECTIVE IDEALISM	110
XI.	OBJECTIVE IDEALISM	119
XII.	OUR KNOWLEDGE OF THE WORLD	134
XIII.	OBJECTIONS TO PERCEPTIONISM. DIFFICULTIES OF REALISM	147
XIV.	TWO CONTEMPORARY AMERICAN THEORIES OF REALISM: NEO-REALISM AND CRITICAL REALISM	155
XV.	TRUTH	166
XVI.	THE CRITERION OF TRUTH AND THE ULTIMATE MOTIVE OF CERTITUDE	181
XVII.	THE TRUTH OF KNOWLEDGE	195
XVIII.	THE CAUSES OF ERROR	207
XIX.	CONCLUSION	217
INDEX		221

ELEMENTS OF EPISTEMOLOGY

CHAPTER I

EPISTEMOLOGY, ITS NATURE, DEFINITION, IMPORTANCE, HISTORY

PHILOSOPHY aims at the interpretation of the universe. Its concern is not the universe conceived as fragmentary, or in a piecemeal state, but the universe viewed comprehensively as a whole. It leaves the description of the various aspects of the universe to other branches of knowledge. Furthermore philosophy does not aim at a mere description of the universe. It seeks to interpret and understand the universe. It strives to achieve the meaning of reality and to discern its purpose and value. This is the speculative function of philosophy.

There is a critical aspect to philosophy as well. The sciences are all based on fundamental assumptions, the examination of which does not fall within the field of any of the sciences which utilize them. The physical sciences, for example, all make use of the conceptions, cause, quantity, quality, space, time, and the like, and yet the study of these important and elementary conceptions is not undertaken by any of the sciences. There is evident need of a study which shall analyze and define these concepts which are so basic in the sciences and in daily life. This latter task is undertaken by philosophy; the prosecution of this task is the critical function of philosophy.

What is true of philosophy in general is also true of that branch of philosophy known as epistemology. The subject matter of epistemology is human knowledge. Obviously human knowledge challenges our attention; it offers a fertile field for investigation. All of that immense store of knowledge we have been acquiring since the "buzzing confusion" of our infancy, a store made up of knowledge of the world around us, of mathematical principles, of goodness, of truth, of beauty, of right and wrong, of ourselves, demands our attention in proportion with the significance this knowledge has for us.

Definition of Epistemology

The word "epistemology" is derived from the Greek words *episteme* (knowledge, science) and *logos* (speech, thought). Its usage as a designation for a specific part of philosophy is comparatively recent.[1] It has gradually supplanted the older names given to this study, such as Applied Logic, Material Logic, Critical Logic, and Noetics. Other terms used synonymously with epistemology are "Theory of Knowledge" and "Criteriology." Strictly speaking there is a difference between the significance of the latter term and that of epistemology. Epistemology has the wider connotation; it is concerned with the knowledge-problem in all its aspects, while criteriology has to do chiefly with the criterion of truth, i.e., the norm or test whereby we distinguish truth from error. The latter is only one of the problems of epistemology. Epistemology may be defined as that branch of philosophy which studies the value or truth of human knowledge. It investigates human knowledge from the standpoint of its validity or truth. It is a philosophic examination of knowledge in an endeavor to enlighten us as to its worth.

The Nature of Epistemology

The nature of epistemology is not easily grasped by the untrained mind. Yet it is of the utmost importance that

[1] Ferrier in his *Institutes of Metaphysics* first popularized it.

the student appreciate the epistemological problem since a proper appreciation of the problem is the first step toward its solution. Thinking goes on in the human mind. Our thoughts are psychic in nature. They are not material objects like stones and trees which are subject to the laws of the physical universe. Yet, among other things, they represent that universe to us. There is an evident gap between the psychic thought and the physical universe which is represented to us through the thought. They are not existentially the same. There are thoughts of things *and* things.

Most of our thoughts are concerned with the external, physical world. The exigencies of life compel us to think about and explain and master our environment. But while we think chiefly of things and events we can think also of our knowledge of things and events. We can think about our thoughts. Knowledge, in other words, may form the subject-matter of a detailed study just as well as the objects in the world about us, and when so studied it gives rise to epistemology. This is the constructive aspect of epistemology—the study of knowledge as knowledge.

In its critical aspect epistemology scrutinizes the presuppositions upon which all our certain knowledge is based. The sciences have admittedly achieved a vast number of conclusions which are true. Yet the obvious postulate of all the sciences, as well as all branches of philosophy, is that true and valid knowledge is attainable and has been attained. But this broad and basic postulate as to the worth of supposedly true knowledge has not been investigated by any of the sciences or by any part of the philosophic discipline. The worth of knowledge, presupposed by them all, does not fall within the scope of any of them. Physics, chemistry, and biology, for example, claim to give us true knowledge, or facts, about their various fields. But they do not inquire into the fact of knowledge itself. They take the validity of knowledge for granted. The same is true of all the sciences. The only branch of knowledge which treats of the question of the truth of knowledge is epistemology.

THE IMPORTANCE OF EPISTEMOLOGY

Since epistemology is an examination of the truth-value of knowledge its importance cannot be gainsaid. The worth of all the sciences, physical and moral, and of all philosophy, depends on the worth of knowledge. If knowledge is untrustworthy the sciences and philosophy are worthless. On the contrary, if we can justify the worth of knowledge science and philosophy retain their validity.

Like the piles that are driven down deep below the surface of the water, unseen but necessary supports, the theory of knowledge upholds all. Whatever we attempt within the whole vast range of the theoretical or practical sciences, all depends ultimately upon our solution of the problem of knowledge.[2]

Again, a man's philosophy of life is determined by his solution of this problem. If skepticism or agnosticism is the outcome of one's study in this subject he cannot be a Christian. Religion and epistemology are linked together inseparably. This does not mean, however, that our study will be undertaken as a defense of, or a preparation for, our faith. Epistemology is not a religious polemic; it is a branch of philosophy and as such must be grounded on reason alone. Our investigation of knowledge must be impartial and disinterested. We cannot appeal to religion in support of our findings since we approach the subject not as theologians but as philosophers.

HISTORY OF EPISTEMOLOGY

The critical investigation of knowledge may be said to be as old as philosophy itself, although epistemology as a dis-

[2] Vance, *Reality and Truth*, p. vii.

ELEMENTS OF EPISTEMOLOGY

tinct branch of philosophy did not appear until modern times.

Ancient Philosophy. In Greece the Eleatics could not reconcile the nature of being as conceived by abstract thought with being as revealed by the senses. Heraclitus could not bridge the same gap. The later Ionians and Atomists were at variance with both these schools, and the upshot of these conflicting theories was the rise of the Sophists who questioned the possibility of certitude and introduced skepticism. Socrates, Plato, and Aristotle maintained against skepticism the power of the mind to attain truth, and they examined the conditions requisite for the attainment of true knowledge. Stoicism and Epicureanism, warring both with each other and with the Academy and the Lyceum, paved the way for a resurgence of skepticism under Pyrrho, Aenesidemus, Sextus Empiricus, and the Middle Academy. But none of these schools treated epistemological problems on their own merits, nor did they mark them off from logical or metaphysical inquiries.

Medieval Philosophy. Two epistemological problems forced themselves to the fore in this period, viz., the harmonizing of the functions of the senses and the intellect in the genesis of knowledge, and the harmonizing of human knowledge with revealed truth. The former of these questions gave rise to the lengthy discussion on the origin and worth of the universals. But the schoolmen, like the Greeks, did not treat epistemology as a separate science. They wrote much on its various questions. They held to the trustworthiness of the senses and the intellect; they insisted on the ability of the mind to achieve certitude; they discussed the conditions of knowledge, but they never articulated their treatises on this subject into a systematic body of doctrine. And this was because the problem, as we know it to-day, had not yet arisen.

Modern Philosophy. The first representative of modern thought, Descartes, by his famous methodic doubt, gave the initial impetus to the modern treatment of the problem of knowledge—the impetus which led to the development of epistemology as a distinct part of philosophy. John Locke in his *Essay concerning Human Understanding* placed the problem of knowledge definitely before thinking minds.

> It came to my thoughts that . . . before we set ourselves upon inquiries of that nature, it was necessary to examine our own abilities, and to see what objects our understandings were, or were not, fitted to deal with. [His intention was to discover] the certainty, evidence, and extent [of human knowledge, to find] the horizon which sets the bounds between the enlightened and dark parts of things, between what is, and what is not, comprehensible by us.[3]

He insisted that we must examine the possibility and value of knowledge before we can assume that knowledge is valid. His own solution of the problem was incorrect but his line of thought was developed by Berkeley and Hume. The latter came to the conclusion that the knowing subject cannot transcend himself in the process of cognition, and that all knowledge can be reduced to sense impressions. Immanuel Kant, roused from his "dogmatic slumber" by Hume's contentions, took up again the problem of the extent, limits, and validity of our knowledge. His solution, briefly stated, is this: the mind can know the phenomena (things as they appear) but it can never attain, because of its constitution, to the noumena (things in themselves). His followers developed his theory of knowledge into a theory of reality.

Our day has seen new attempts to solve this problem, some of these attempts being restatements of older solu-

---

[3] *Essay concerning Human Understanding,* Preface to the Reader.

tions, while others are substantially new. To-day epistemology stands in the forefront of the philosophical sciences. While the preceding summary shows it was the last among them to receive a separate and systematic treatment, it has in our time won for itself a place of prime importance. It may be said that the distinguishing characteristic of the philosophic thought of our age is the dominance of the problem of knowledge. The past few years have witnessed a searching analysis of the cognitive powers of the mind, and the results of this study cannot be ignored by anyone who aspires to a knowledge of philosophy.

Relation of Epistemology to Logic and Psychology

The place which epistemology holds in relation to the other branches of philosophy may be seen from the following diagram:

Philosophy
- Speculative
  - General Metaphysics
    - Ontology, the science of being
    - Epistemology, the science of knowledge
  - Special Metaphysics
    - Cosmology
    - Psychology
    - Natural Theology
- Practical
  - Logic
  - Ethics

The two branches of philosophy with which epistemology is most closely linked are logic and psychology. A delineation of the differences between epistemology and logic, on the one hand, and between epistemology and psychology on the other, will serve to bring out the character of epistemology into sharper relief. The chief concern of logic is to secure clearness and consistency in our ideas and correctness in our reasoning. The canons of logic guarantee the truth of the conclusion of a reasoning process only hypothetically, i.e., granting among other things that truth and certitude are attainable. These assumptions of logic devolve upon our study. Epistemology differs from psychology both in its material and formal objects. The material object of psychology is wider than that of our study, embracing, as it does, the soul and all its states, whether cognitive, volitional, or emotional. Epistemology has to do only with the cognitional states of the mind. Moreover psychology considers the cognitive states of the mind as facts or mental events, while these same activities engage the attention of the epistemology only in so far as they purport to be true. Psychology deals with thinking as a fact, while epistemology deals rather with the purpose or goal or meaning of the fact.

An illustration may clarify this point. Let us take as an example this syllogism:

All buildings which conform to the norm of beauty are beautiful.
The Capitol at Washington conforms to the norm of beauty.
Therefore the Capitol at Washington is beautiful.

The logician confronted with this syllogism inquires whether it is consistent or not. He asks the question, "Does the conclusion follow logically from the premises?" and if it does he pronounces it to be a correct syllogism. The psychologist is not concerned with its consistency. He is concerned rather with the genesis of the concepts "building," "norm," "beautiful," etc., and with the questions how we sense the Capitol and the like. The epistemologist confines his attention to the truth of the above propositions. He asks, "Can we make these assertions with certainty?" "Have we any warrant for them?" "Is our perception of the Capitol true?" "Are the concepts found in the syllogism valid interpretations of reality?" Psychology, in a word, attempts to answer the question, "How do we know?" while epistemology attempts to answer the question, "Is our knowledge true?"

Definition of Terms

Knowledge. Knowledge, since it is a primitive fact of consciousness cannot be defined. We can examine it and describe it, but we cannot resolve it into simpler elements, nor can we state it in terms of anything else. "Knowledge is *sui generis*. . . . Knowledge is simply knowledge, and any attempt to state it in terms of something else must end in describing something which is not knowledge." [4]

But our inability to define knowledge does not prevent our knowing what it is, and nothing is clearer to us than the nature of knowledge. Besides a definition could be of value only in so far as it was known, i.e., only in so far as it implied a knowledge of the thing to be defined. To know is to be aware of something. An object is known when it is present to a knowing consciousness. When I know this book it is present to me; not, however, in the way in which it is present in the material world. In that world it retains its own physical existence. But it has also, when known, an additional existence, i.e., an existence in my mind.[5] A knowing being is thus enriched by the mental possession of something other than itself. In this it is differentiated from non-knowing beings. The latter have only their own reality while the former is capable of the cognitive possession of other realities.[6]

We cannot know without knowing something, and this latter is the object of knowledge. The object of knowledge may be anything, a material object, a fact, or a general prin-

---

[4] Prichard, *Kant's Theory of Knowledge*, p. 124; see also p. 245.
[5] St. Thomas, *Summa Theologica*, 1, q. 14, art. 1.
[6] St. Thomas, *"De Veritate,"* q. 23, art. 1; in lib. *De Anima*, 1, q. 9.

ciple; anything, in brief, that can fall within the range of our knowledge. It may be external or internal, i.e., we can know not only reality which is external to the mind, but we can also know the states of the mind itself, such as our emotions, feelings, and thoughts. But whatever we know must be present within the knowing mind. Knowledge always implies the antithesis of the mind and the object, and it also implies the relation or presence of the object to the mind.

Further insight into the meaning of knowledge may be gained from a consideration of the different meanings of the verb "to know." When I say, "I know this man," I may mean that I have seen him and that I would recognize him again. This is knowledge of acquaintance; it implies that I myself have directly perceived the man. Or my "knowing" may mean that I understand him; that I know his hidden and deeper qualities. This knowledge may be direct or indirect, as I may know a man in this sense although I have never seen him. Hence "to know" may mean either to perceive and apprehend, or to understand and comprehend.[7]

Cognition is sometimes used as a synonym for knowledge, but strictly speaking it means the act or process of knowing —knowledge being the result of this process. In the same way knowledge is sometimes used to designate the process of knowing and sometimes the object known. Thus I may speak of my knowledge of physics, and of the science of physics as a body of knowledge.

Experience. Experience is a term used to designate a phase of conscious life which an individual undergoes. It sometimes stands for practical knowledge gained through per-

---

[7] In many languages this difference of meanings of the verb "to know" is expressed by the use of two verbs instead of the one used in English, e.g., *cognoscere* and *scire* in Latin; *gnonai* and *eidenai* in Greek; *kennen* and *wissen* in German; see James, *Principles of Psychology*, Vol. I, p. 221.

sonal acquaintance—through impressions made upon one directly. It is thus opposed to knowledge gained through description, or to knowledge which is not direct but secondhand. When we say, "I had an experience," we mean that we ourselves received a direct impression of some kind. Sometimes it stands for the fruit of knowledge which is so obtained. One who has attained a certain proficiency or wisdom through repeated experiences is said to be a man of experience. So we speak of an experienced statesman or an experienced soldier. In epistemology when we speak of experience or of experiential knowledge we mean knowledge gained through the senses.

Science. Science is a particular kind of knowledge. Knowledge which has been arranged in order and systematized is called scientific. It is opposed to promiscuous and unorganized knowledge. The average man has some knowledge of the facts with which physics deals, but unless he has studied the science of physics his knowledge would not be considered scientific, since he has not correlated the facts of physics and organized them into a coherent body of doctrine. When knowledge has been systematized it forms what are called the sciences.

Belief. Belief is the acceptance of something on the authority of another. It is therefore a kind of knowledge. When we assent to a judgment because we are convinced of its truth, and our conviction is not based on the word of another we are said to have scientific knowledge, but when the motive of our assent is the word of another we are said to believe. We must note, however, that if our authority is trustworthy, our belief affords us true knowledge. It frequently happens that we assent to judgments for which the evidence is not compelling or irresistible, but for which the evidence seems sufficient for rational assent. In such cases we are said to "believe" in these judgments, and a distinction is made between our assent to them and our assent to judgments we "know." But here too our belief is knowledge. In ordinary speech men use "belief" of those judgments of which they are uncertain, and "knowledge" of those judgments to which they adhere with certitude. Thus we hear, "I don't know whether it is true or not, but I believe it." In this usage belief is distinguished from knowledge as is opinion from certitude.[8]

Consciousness. Consciousness, like thought, cannot be defined. In its widest sense it denotes all our sensations, thoughts, feelings, and volitions—in brief all our mental life. We are conscious of our mental states when we are aware of them. Self-consciousness means the mind's consciousness of its operations as its own. It thus designates only the cognitive activity of the mind. Self-consciousness is of two kinds, direct and reflex. Direct (or spontaneous) self-consciousness is a hazy, confused knowledge of the fact that we are aware of something. Reflex self-consciousness is an explicit, formal examination or consideration of our mental states. When I simply know something without explicitly adverting to the fact that I know, my self-consciousness is direct. But when I purposely make my knowledge of this something an object of my knowledge, when I distinctly and explicitly consider the acts or states of my mind for the purpose of examining them, my self-consciousness is reflex. The form of mental activity by which I look into my own mind and its states, or by which I "bend" my mind back upon itself, is called introspection or reflection.

Intellect. By intellect is meant the higher faculty of thought. We have two kinds of knowledge, sense knowledge and intellectual knowledge. This distinction we shall

---

[8] The definition of belief as a form of knowledge is made necessary by the post-Kantian tendency to regard belief as a form of knowledge not acquired by the intellect—or knowledge not based on intellectual grounds.

attempt to justify later, only indicating the distinction here.*
The term intellect is loosely used. Sometimes the intellect is
called the reason. The latter term is often used to designate
the intellect when it is basing its judgments on intrinsic
evidence rather than on authority. In its narrower and more
correct denotation, however, reason means the discursive or
inferential faculty, i.e., the faculty whereby we infer conclusions. This is the significance it has in the statement,
"Man is a rational animal."

* See pp. 56, 86.

CHAPTER II

THE INITIAL ATTITUDE TOWARD KNOWLEDGE. THE METHOD AND DATA OF EPISTEMOLOGY

Reflective Thinking

EPISTEMOLOGY is a study which has emerged within the sphere of a complex experience, and which is born of reflection on the worth of knowledge. It must be noted that not all thinking is reflective. An analysis of the mental states which are called "thought" shows that many of them are by no means reflective. Thinking may be casual and undirected; it may pursue a rambling course and it may not be concerned with the solution of a problem. Ideas may flow at random through the mind. Sometimes mental activity is taken up with the appreciation of the beautiful. It may be a response to the æsthetic appeal of some beautiful object in the world around us. Occasionally thoughts are the means of constructing a tale which has no pretense of being true, but which must possess congruity. None of these kinds of thought is reflective. Thinking is reflective when it is concerned with solving a problem, when it is endeavoring to discern the significance of a perplexing situation, when it is attempting to attain a true conclusion. Reflective thinking is "active, persistent and careful consideration of any belief or supposed form of knowledge in the light of the grounds that tend to support it, and the further conclusions to which it tends." [1]

It is clear that epistemology is born of reflective thinking

[1] Dewey, *How We Think*, p. 6.

about thought because it is an attempt to solve the problem of knowledge and to arrive at a true conclusion as to the worth of knowledge.

Kinds of Cognitive States. An inventory of the states of mind which occur in reflective thinking, viewed from the standpoint of firmness of adherence to what we believe to be true, shows that they vary considerably. There is, first of all, the state of ignorance or nescience—a partial or total lack of knowledge. There is also the state of doubt. It sometimes happens that affirmation and negation of a judgment are both impossible, due to the lack of evidence for or against a proposition. In this state my mind remains in suspense. Another state of mind I frequently have is that of opinion. In this state my mind assents to a judgment, but with a lurking fear that it may be wrong in so doing. It is inclined to accept the judgment, and it does so provisionally because there are weightier reasons for than against it. But the motives for assent are inconclusive and hence the assent is not fixed and firm. Reflection reveals still another state of mind differing from both doubt and opinion. This is the state of certitude or conviction. It is the state (or act) of the mind in which the mind assents to a judgment as true without fear of error. When the reasons for the judgment are convincing and conclusive, and when all prudent fear of error is excluded, the mind is certain.

Not only do I have convictions but it is patent that other men have them as well. They often use the words "certain" and "certitude," or their equivalents, in the same sense that I use them. Their actions evidence the fact that they have convictions. They eat, drink, step out of the way of moving vehicles, take trains, etc., plainly manifesting thereby that they are acting on a knowledge they believe to be certain.[2]

[2] Epistemology is concerned only with our convictions because they alone are thought to be indisputably true.

Certitude is no guarantee of truth. Some authors hold that truth is necessarily conjoined with conviction. They claim that all judgments of which we are certain are true. Others maintain that we can and do have false certitudes. Common usage favors the second opinion, for the term "certitude" is applied to all assents whether true or false. It is a fact that we often assent to false judgments and that when we so assent we are not aware of any difference between such assents and the assent we give to true judgments.

The history of the sciences shows us that many theories have been held as indisputably true which were afterwards discarded. We may cite as examples former beliefs in the geocentric theory, in the impossibility of the antipodes, and in spontaneous generation. The same is true in the fields of history, philosophy, and religion. Not only have men been mistaken in the past but there are many erroneous certitudes to which credence is given to-day. The contradictory views entertained in all fields of knowledge offer a clear proof that some of these views are wrong, notwithstanding the fact that they are professed with a tenacity that would seem to indicate conviction. But we do not have to appeal to the experience of the race to prove that firmness of conviction is not necessarily a mark of truth. A candid scrutiny of our own mental life makes clear the fact that we have often been convinced of the truth of many judgments and that we have afterwards been forced to discard or revise them because new experience, new information, etc., proved them to be false.

The fact that certitude and truth have not been and are not necessarily conjoined gives rise to the epistemological problem. All that purports to be true knowledge is not true knowledge. Our conviction that our certain knowledge is true does not make it true. Were human thought always in conformity with the facts the problem of knowledge would never have arisen. In our daily lives when things run evenly there is very little reflective thinking, simply because the problems which evoke reflection are absent. Reflective thinking requires a cause, which in this instance is the lack of harmony between our knowledge and reality. As long as an automobile is in perfect running order we are not concerned with its mechanism. But if it refuses to run we become interested in the mechanism at once. Similarly when we find obstacles which prevent the practical application of our supposed knowledge, when some of our certitudes contradict others, what more natural than that we begin a study of knowledge with the aim of discovering whether or not its claim to truth is justified. Is any of our knowledge true? Do my perceptions represent the world of reality to me truly? Are not my perceptions, which seem to be perceptions of reality, merely private mental experiences of my own mind which do not represent extramental reality at all? Is there any extramental reality? Is there any test or norm or standard which will enable me to discern truth from error? What, if any, are the limits to knowledge? These are a few of the many questions which present themselves to reflective thought for solution. Our own errors and the clash of our convictions with the convictions of others beget doubt, and this gives rise to reflection on the value of knowledge.

The epistemological problem thus emerges in the race and in the individual as soon as men begin to reflect on knowledge. In the beginning knowledge is no problem. Its validity is taken for granted. It is not concerned with itself or with its processes. Rational reflection turns on itself last of all. At first men look outward. Their knowledge is concerned with the objective because it is the objective they seek to explain. In course of time difficulties in the practical application of knowledge arise and it is only then they begin to ponder the knowledge-problem. When the fruits of their reflection on the question of knowledge were articulated into a coherent body of doctrine epistemology became a separate part of the philosophic discipline.

The Initial Attitude toward Knowledge

It is of the utmost importance that we adopt the correct attitude toward knowledge at the outset of our study. Many theories of knowledge have been vitiated because they approached the subject of knowledge from the wrong standpoint. The problem of knowledge should, first of all, be approached with an open mind. It is the object of every science to come to some definite conclusions about its subject matter, which conclusions it coördinates into systematic form. If it is to arrive at the truth about its subject-matter it must view this latter in a detached, impersonal way. The student of knowledge must purge his mind of all bias which he may have hitherto had. He must examine knowledge as it is, not as he thinks it should be, nor as he wishes it to be. Personal preference must be eliminated. His conclusions as to the worth of knowledge must not be shaped so as to fit into a preconceived philosophical theory. He must fit his philosophical theory to his findings on the subject of knowledge. The philosopher, and especially the epistemologist, should practice in this regard the same renunciation, the same rigor of procedure, that distinguishes the true scientist. It is a commonplace that those who look for a preconceived theory in the field of knowledge will probably find it. Hope and expectation almost inevitably distort our intellectual vision. We should, if we want the truth about knowledge, be prepared to accept the defeat of expectations, and we should never confuse our hopes with the facts.

The history of philosophy shows us that the viewpoints of philosophers on the question of knowledge may be divided into two classes: (1) Dogmatism, and (2) Skepticism. The former theory holds that the problem of knowledge is capable of being solved, while the latter maintains that it is insoluble.

The Correct Attitude

In common with most thinkers we shall profess a species of dogmatism. We shall not summarily rule the claims of skepticism out of court. But we believe, for reasons we shall give, that the arguments adduced by the skeptics impugning the validity of knowledge are not a sufficient motive for our abandoning the dogmatic view.[3]

Ultra-dogmatism. The term "dogmatism" is in bad repute in philosophy, and to guard against any criticism of our "dogmatic" attitude a distinction must be made. There are two kinds of dogmatism, ultra-dogmatism and critical dogmatism. By the former is meant an epistemology which is based on assumptions which are unproven and which are held to be above the necessity of philosophical examination. The ultra-dogmatist insists that we must accept as established the fact of knowledge and the ability of the mind to know the truth. He bases his view on two arguments: (a) We cannot doubt the aptitude of the mind to attain the truth since we suppose it in our very beliefs on this question. (b) If our epistemological inquiry begins with a doubt as to the mind's ability to know the truth we can never get beyond this doubt; none of our conclusions can be certain since they are grounded on this uncertainty. A theory of knowledge is knowledge, and hence it assumes the validity of the very thing it seeks to establish.

We answer that if we presuppose as an established fact the ability of the mind to know the truth we commit a *petitio principii* for we are assuming the very thing which is to be proved. As to the first argument, it is true that we are using the same faculty we are testing, but we do so

[3] See below, p. 29.

because it is the only instrument at our command. We must use the mind to test the mind. But this does not necessitate our postulating its powers to know the truth as a philosophically established certitude.[4]

Our procedure is this: we start with an initial spontaneous assumption that the mind can know the truth. We use the mind in the process of examining spontaneous certitudes and we are thus enabled to decide whether our spontaneous belief in its worth is justified or not. To those who maintain that we cannot even presuppose the power of the mind to know the truth as a spontaneous certitude we reply that were we to abandon this certitude all thought would be paralyzed, and it would be impossible to prosecute any search into the truth of knowledge. We cannot construct any theory of knowledge unless we use our minds—but we do not have to begin our study with the initial assumption that it is philosophically certain that our minds are trustworthy.[5]

Critical Dogmatism. The critical attitude is that the science of epistemology cannot be erected on a basis of untested assumptions, that nothing in that science must be taken for granted. If the critical dogmatist makes assumptions, as he is forced to do by the nature of his problem, he is willing to subject them to a critical examination. He knows that skepticism usually centers its attacks on the unwarranted assumptions of dogmatism, and that the questions as to the worth of knowledge cannot be solved by claiming exemption from scrutiny for certain spontaneous convictions. He is therefore willing to give ear to the claims of those who hold that the mind is an unreliable guide to truth. He does not prejudge the issue.

[4] A spontaneous certitude is one assented to without a critical examination. When the motives for assent are weighed, this certitude, if it is found to be justified, becomes a philosophic certitude.

[5] See Coffey, *Epistemology*, Vol. I, pp. 90-109; Walker, *Theories of Knowledge*, p. 623; Jeannière, *Criterologia*, p. 108; Vance, *op. cit.*, p. 56.

Critical dogmatism therefore holds that the correct state of mind in which the problem should be approached is that of universal methodic doubt. Doubt, as we have seen, is a state of mind in which the mind refuses assent to a proposition or to its contrary because of the lack of sufficient evidence for either. A universal doubt is one so wide in extent that it embraces all our convictions. A methodic doubt is one that is voluntarily induced for the purpose of obtaining further knowledge. It is a matter of choice; it is freely entertained; it is not forced upon one. Thus if I regard a conviction for the time being as if it were doubtful so that I can go over the grounds of my assent to it and also the difficulties against it, I doubt it methodically. This doubt differs from real doubt which is not voluntary but which is forced upon us by evidence which prevents the mind's assent.

Our doubt must be universal; we must exempt none of our convictions from investigation. The object of epistemology is to subject to examination all our spontaneous certitudes. If we consider any of them to be above the necessity of examination and immune from criticism they cannot become philosophic certitudes. A mere affirmation will not make them such; nor will it settle the question as to their truth. Others, the skeptics for example, will deny their truth, and the question will remain unsettled. The only way in which we can make any headway against our opponents is to go over all our certain judgments to see if they stand the test of critical reflection.

Our doubt must be methodic; we must consider all our convictions as if they were doubtful. It is obvious that we can methodically doubt only such of our judgments as we believe to be true. But the question arises: can we doubt all our spontaneous convictions? As regards our freely formed convictions all agree that we can methodically doubt them. The difficulty lies in our apparent inability to doubt irresistible, or immediately evident convictions, convictions such as "two and two equal four," and "I am reading." It seems that the evidence of such judgments is too cogent to permit of our doubting them even methodically. But some philosophers have denied the power of the mind to know the truth. Hence to meet the contentions of these thinkers we must methodically doubt this power of the mind. It is the only way in which we can argue with them; we cannot dismiss their arguments with a mere denial. But this doubt about the mind's capacity to attain the truth involves a doubt as to all the cognitive acts of the mind, and therefore as to the objectivity of self-evident judgments as well. We cannot really doubt these judgments since they compel our assent, but we can doubt their objectivity. Does the fact that I am forced to admit them prove they are true? Is their psychological necessity a proof of their objective necessity? I believe they are objectively true, but for the purpose of investigation I methodically doubt them. I can consider the objections of those who claim they are only subjectively necessary. We must bear in mind that the objectivity of self-evident judgments is one of the main problems of epistemology. There are those who claim that the necessity of these judgments is due to the constitution of the mind or to subjective propensities. May we not hold that these certitudes are open to investigation in order that we may perhaps vindicate their objectivity? It would seem that we can and must extend our methodic doubt even to self-evident judgments, i.e., we may and must methodically doubt their relation to reality. But we must, at the same time, bear in mind that there is a world of difference between real doubt and methodic doubt.

Methodic doubt has been employed for centuries in argumentation. Indirect proof, or the *reductio ad impossibile,* is an example of it. It has been utilized by Euclid, Aristotle, St. Augustine, and others. In the Middle Ages the teachers formulated their theses as questions, not that they really doubted what they questioned, but simply to afford an easy way for the stating and refuting of the objections against their position. When St. Thomas, for example, asks, "Does God exist?" he does not really doubt the existence of God; he is for the moment considering it to be an open question so that he can the more conveniently prove his point and expose the arguments of his opponents.

THE DATA OF EPISTEMOLOGY

In conformity with the tenets of critical dogmatism it is evident that epistemology has as its data: (1) our spontaneous convictions, and (2) the power of reflection. The existence of spontaneous convictions cannot be doubted. Even skeptics admit that we have them.[6] From our earliest years we have yielded unquestioning assent to a great many facts, principles, and the like. We are therefore basing our inquiry on a fact admitted by all philosophers and we do not draw the censure even of the skeptics, because it is not the fact of certain knowledge that is in question but its significance, as we shall see. Should anyone dogmatically deny the fact of certain knowledge he disproves the truth of his assertion by the assertion itself, for he knows one thing at least, viz., that he does not know. Should he doubt the fact of certain knowledge he puts himself beyond the range of discussion.

As to the power of reflection, i.e., our ability to reflect upon our mental states, to examine them, and to go over the grounds of our assent, this also is a fact. The existence of this unique power of the mind is proved by its functioning. Moreover it is the only instrument we have which enables us to test our certitudes.

[6] See Hume, *Treatise on Human Nature*, Green and Grose, Vol. I, p. 548.

The Method of Epistemology

The method to be followed in this study is the subjection of our spontaneous certitudes to the testing of reflection. Those certitudes which survive the rigorous analysis of reflection will be retained as true. Those which cannot satisfy the demands of reflection will be discarded. We will make a deliberate introspective study of our spontaneous convictions, not in as much as they are mental facts—this is the work of psychology—but in as much as they claim to be true. Our introspection must be systematic and scientific. It must differ in extent and intensity and method from the reflections of the man in the street whose reflections on his spontaneous assents are, as a rule, unsystematic and haphazard. Care must be taken in reflecting on our mental processes that we retain an unprejudiced and unbiased attitude. The wish of the philosopher is often father to his thought, and we must guard against permitting our prejudices to influence the findings of introspection. It is easy to discover what we are looking for because of unconscious autosuggestion, and this will happen unless we are honest and detached in reporting the contents of our mind.

This is but another way of saying that our philosophizing on the theory of knowledge will be futile unless we are willing at the outset of our study to abide by the facts. Epistemology springs from experience and it must be tested by experience. As we review various theories advanced by some of the more prominent philosophers on the mooted questions of epistemology we shall employ this test more than any other, viz., do these theories square with all the relevant facts?

The Method of Descartes. René Descartes (1596-1650) introduced a method into philosophy which, while no longer held, is because of its fame deserving of mention. He was keenly aware of the errors and contradictions of his contemporaries and of preceding thinkers, and to avoid skepticism he undertook to construct a new philosophy which would have none of the faults of other systems of thought. To avoid the errors which had marred other philosophies he determined to make a clean slate of his mind. He would rid himself of all opinions and convictions acquired from books, education, and from the testimony of his senses and his intellect. He would deliberately doubt everything. Having thus emptied his mind, he would start anew from a firm, true basis and on this he would erect a philosophy which would not be encumbered by the errors of the past. After he had rid himself of all persuasions which doubt had succeeded in unsettling he had left only one truth which he could not doubt. This surviving certitude is that he, the thinker, exists. As he phrased it, "I think, therefore I am." His own existence is the basic certitude which alone is saved from the wreckage of doubt. It is the "unshakeable rock" on which can be built a system of thought which will be indisputably true.[7]

There is considerable controversy as to the nature of Descartes' doubt. It seems to be a real doubt, entertained, as he says, "for strong and serious reasons." A doubt which is real, and which is as all-embracing as his, extends to the possibility of the mind to know the truth. This doubt should have destroyed the value of his whole system. Logically he should have become a skeptic. But he claimed to be able to doubt mathematical propositions and even the principle of contradiction. It seems impossible for one really to doubt these since they compel our assent. Hence we must interpret him in another way. We can understand that while he could not have really doubted these irresistible convictions, he

[7] See his *Discours de la Méthode*. Descartes explicitly excluded from his doubt the truths of theology and the political and moral sciences.

could have really doubted that they gave him any insight into reality—he could have doubted that they were objective. On this interpretation of his doubt what is the value of his method?

If Descartes accepted self-evident principles only in a subjective sense, and if he really doubted their giving him any information about the extra-subjective order, then logically he should have attached the same subjective significance to his "I think, therefore I am." It is not logical to single out this judgment from all other self-evident judgments and claim objectivity and truth for it, and to deny the latter to all other similar judgments. The force of the other irresistible convictions is just as compelling and cogent as the force of the "I think." It must stand or fall with all other self-evident judgments. If objectivity is granted to the one it must be granted to the others. And if he doubted the testimony of all the acts of consciousness, for the same reason he should have doubted its testimony when it assured him of his existence.[8]

[8] See Mercier, *Crit. Gener.*, p. 80.

CHAPTER III

THE NATURE OF JUDGMENT. SKEPTICISM

It has been said above that we are to examine the truth-claim of our spontaneous convictions. They seem to be objective and true, i.e., they seem to refer to reality, and they apparently represent reality as it is. The question of the objectivity and truth of our convictions seems idle to the man in the street. He takes for granted that when he makes a judgment of whose truth he is convinced that his judgment refers truly to the reality of which it is made. For example, when he enunciates the judgment, "This paper is white," he does not mean that his judgment is a mere comparison of two mental states, his idea of paper and his idea of white. He thinks that his judgment has a true objective reference, i.e., that there is a reality called paper, and that it is really white.[1]

But, as we shall see, this question of the objectivity and truth of our convictions is not as simple as it appears at first glance. In fact it is one of the most disputed questions in our study.

Our convictions are formulated in judgments. Hence the question of the objectivity and truth of our convictions resolves itself into the question of the objectivity and truth of our certain judgments. A certain judgment is a judgment made up of two ideas (in the broad sense of that term)

[1] "Objective" in epistemology means that which pertains to the object known, whether the latter is intra- or extra-subjective. "Subject" means the knower as knowing, as undergoing a cognitive experience, while "subjective" signifies what belongs to the knowing subject as such.

which are present to the mind, the identity of which is affirmed or denied without any fear of error. An analysis of certain judgments reveals to us their three constitutive elements: (1) two ideas, (2) the nexus between them, (3) the certain affirmation or denial of one of the ideas of the other.

Kinds of Judgments

There are two bases of division as regards judgments: (1) difference in the ideas, and (2) difference in the nexus or synthesis between the ideas.

Viewed from the standpoint of difference in the ideas, judgments are: (a) Of the ideal order, when the subject and predicate are abstract. In this case the truth enunciated in the judgment is said to be an abstract truth, or a truth of the ideal order. An example of an abstract truth is: man is a rational animal. (b) Of the real order, when the subject of the judgment is concrete. In this case the truth enunciated is said to be a concrete truth, or a truth of the real order. "John is ill" is a concrete truth.

Viewed from the standpoint of a difference in the nexus, judgments are either: (a) Absolutely necessary, analytic, or a priori, if the nexus or connection between the subject and predicate is necessary, i.e., independent of all conditions and hence universal. On no condition can the judgment be other than it is; it can never be false while its contradictory must always be false. In these judgments the nexus becomes known by a mere analysis and comparison of the subject and predicate. An example: the whole is greater than any of its parts. (b) Hypothetically necessary, synthetic, or a posteriori, if the nexus depends on a condition, and is therefore contingent or non-necessary. In judgments of this kind the nexus is known only by experience, e.g., bodies tend downwards.

Bearing these distinctions in mind we can now approach

the problems of epistemology proper. These problems fall into two main groups: (1) *the problem of the origin of knowledge*, (2) *the problem of the worth of knowledge*. Whence come our certain judgments, and what is their worth? These two questions epistemology must answer. The worth of knowledge may depend upon its origin. Hence the question of the origin of knowledge must be answered before we can take up the question of the validity of knowledge. Knowledge must present its credentials before it can be evaluated. We shall, therefore, first study the origin of our convictions. Having answered that question we shall be in a position to discuss the value of knowledge. But before either of these problems can be taken up the claims of skepticism, that school which holds that our convictions cannot be philosophically justified, must be examined.

Skepticism

Definition of Skepticism. The term "skepticism" is derived form the Greek *skeptesthai* which means to inquire, to examine carefully. A skeptic in the broad sense is one who is in search of truth; he is an inquirer, one who has not made up his mind, who is undecided.

Kinds of Skepticism. In the philosophic sense skepticism stands for (1) doubt based on rational grounds, (2) disbelief based on the same grounds, (3) a denial of the possibility of the attainment of truth. The last is philosophical skepticism in the strict sense of the term, and it is this with which we are concerned.

Philosophical skepticism is then the doctrine which doubts or denies that the human mind can know the truth. It may be (a) subjective (or absolute), i.e., a skepticism which doubts absolutely everything, even states of consciousness, or (b) objective (or relative). Skeptics of this kind admit the existence of certain judgments as psychological facts but they doubt that they have objective validity. The skeptic of history is of this latter type.

Objective skepticism, looked at from the standpoint of its extension, is of two kinds: (a) universal, i.e., it doubts the validity of all convictions no matter what their source, and (b) partial, i.e., it doubts only the validity of some convictions, viz., those derived from particular sources. Fideism, for example, doubts the worth of natural knowledge but believes in the worth of supernatural knowledge.

A partial list of the better known skeptics of history contains the following: In Greek philosophy, Protagoras, Gorgias, Pyrrho, Aenesidemus, Arcesilaus, Carneades, Sextus Empiricus. In more modern times: Montaigne, Charron, Sanchez, Huet, Pascal, Bayle, Hume, Jouffroy, Balfour. Most of the moderns are partial skeptics: they restrict unduly the power of the mind but they do not believe we should remain in a state of doubt. They thus escape skepticism by making non-rational grounds the basis of certitude.

An Examination of Skepticism. Our position is in brief that the arguments adduced by the skeptics are invalid.

First argument. This argument is based on the history of human thought. The innumerable errors which have always prevailed and which still prevail show the utter unreliability of the human mind. The history of thought is but the sad tale of man's endeavor to know the truth and of his failures to attain his goal. After all the centuries of mental travail men still disagree on fundamental questions in philosophy, religion, and in other fields of knowledge. Everywhere we see a hopeless diversity of beliefs even among the intellectuals. Especially is this true of philosophy. The theories which divided Greek thought into opposing camps have persisted throughout the history of philosophy to our own day. Democritus and Plato and Aristotle have their modern counterparts. If the mind, say the skeptics, were capable of discovering the truth it would have done so long ago, and at least some of the interminable discussions of philosophy would have been ended.

CRITICISM: The existence of error is a fact—as is the existence of controversy. But, in the first place, the fact that the skeptics claim to know that there is error and conflict of opinion implies that the mind can know at least one thing with certitude, viz., the existence of error and conflict. Again, error is the absence or lack of truth, the lack of conformity between a judgment and the reality about which the judgment is made. But this implies that there is such a thing as truth, else there would be no error. It implies, furthermore, that there is a criterion of truth since without a criterion we could never know we were in error. If there were no criterion of truth, if we could not distinguish between truth and error, then skepticism would be inevitable and logical. But the skeptics have not proved, and cannot prove that there is no such test. The existence of error does not prove that the mind is radically deceptive; it indicates rather that the quest of knowledge has many pitfalls, that reason is not necessarily infallible, and that we are all liable to error.

As to contradictions in thought—their existence is likewise obvious. Not that contradiction is as widespread as the skeptics would have us believe. There are many irresistible convictions which no one denies, such as the immediate data of consciousness and self-evident judgments. But the contradictions which do exist do not prove that the mind is necessarily defective. They prove that the achieving of truth is difficult, and that the search after truth is laborious. Moreover, contradictions are easily accounted for. Ambiguity, misconception, misinterpretation, careless reasoning, malobservation, non-observation, in fact all the causes of error, adequately explain the existence of contradictions. This argument of the skeptics is a *non-sequitur*.

Finally, we should be heartened by the fact that many problems once considered hopeless have been solved. The mind has progressed in knowledge and this progress inspires us with the hope that many problems as yet unsolved will yield to the pressure of time. The conquests of the mind which history reveals to us justify our *ignoramus* but not our *ignorabimus*.

Second argument. The problem of the ultimate nature of reality must ever remain insoluble because of the so-called antinomies. In its interpretation of reality the mind is often restricted to a choice between two theories which are contradictory and yet which must both be false, despite the fact it is logically necessary that one member of a pair of contradictories be true. Hence it seems that a solution of the problem is logically impossible. There are a great many of these antinomies. One of the oldest and most famous is that concerning the existence of local motion. It was first propounded by Zeno the Eleatic and it has lost none of its force through the centuries. Reason tells us that local motion is impossible because it implies the traversing of an infinite number of spatial intervals in a finite time.[2] But the senses tell us that local motion is real. To reject the verdict of our senses is nonsensical, while to reject the pronouncement of our reason is unreasonable. Both cannot be true and yet neither can be true, because of the testimony of the other. This is only one of the many antinomies that suggest themselves. It, together with the others, proves that the conflict between sense and reason is irreconcilable and that consequently the nature of reality is unknowable. The negative attitude of skepticism is therefore the logical one.

[2] For a detailed statement of Zeno's argument see Burnet, *Early Greek Philosophy*, p. 366.

CRITICISM: It is clear that the skeptical attitude is justifiable only if the attempted solutions of the antinomies have been discredited. We believe that these antinomies have been, or can be, solved. Aristotle himself solved the antinomy of Zeno.[3] The other antinomies have also found satisfactory solutions. Should a doubt persist that they cannot be solved we should remember that our inability to offer satisfactory solutions does not mean that solutions are impossible. To say that they are insoluble is one thing, to admit we cannot solve them is another.

Third argument. This is the historic diallēlus propounded by Montaigne.[4]

It may be stated thus: it is impossible to prove, or even to know, the criterion of knowledge, since you must use a criterion to test the worth of any arguments you adduce to prove it, as these arguments are of no value unless tested. But how can this second criterion be valid unless you employ another criterion to test the arguments proving its validity? And so on indefinitely. In other words, each criterion we use stands in need of justification while the supposed criterion needs in turn a justification of its own. In the event we use an untested criterion we are begging the question. Hence, Montaigne argues, any attempt to prove a criterion of knowledge is impaled on the horns of a dilemma, one horn being the infinite regress, the other being the assumption of the thing to be proved.

CRITICISM: This is an awkward objection and it offers a real difficulty to any theory of knowledge which holds to an extrinsic theory of truth. However the criterion of truth is not extrinsic. Hence it seems that the flaw of the diallelus

---

[3] *Phys.*, 6, 9, 24. For a more modern solution see Montague, *The Ways of Knowing*, p. 178; Spaulding, *The New Rationalism*, p. 166. For other antinomies consult Kant's "Transcendental Dialectic," the third part of his *Critique of Pure Reason*.

[4] *Essais*, l. 2, chap. 12.

lies in this assumption, namely that the criterion must always be extrinsic to, and distinct from, the judgment of whose truth it is the test. If we can prove, as we hope to do, that true judgments contain in themselves a characteristic which is the test of their truth, so that we see at the same time the truth of the judgment and its validity, then we escape between the horns of the dilemma Montaigne has set.

Fourth argument. This argument of the skeptics is based on the physical and physiological conditions of perception. Between the sensed object and the perceiving subject there are intervening so many physical and physiological processes that it is impossible for us to acquire a true knowledge of reality. Since a change in one of the factors intervening between the brain and a visual object, for example, will result in a different perception, how can we ever be sure that the mental representation of, and the judgment concerning, an external object corresponds to that external object, which is one, but only one, of the causes of that experience and of that judgment?

CRITICISM: We shall postpone a detailed answer to this argument. Briefly our answer is that the relativity of sensation is not a bar to knowing; it is rather a means of knowledge.[5]

We must also bear in mind that this objection is apposite only to such knowledge as involves the use of the sensory apparatus. It is not relevant as regards knowledge of reality which does not involve the use of our senses. But a more glaring flaw in this argument permits us to dispose of it at once. From premises which assert the validity of that knowledge which makes known to us the mechanism of perception, the skeptic concludes that knowledge is invalid. That very knowledge which is invalid is the knowledge by which he is aware of the existence of ether waves, air, nervous system,

[5] See p. 137.

brain, etc. From premises which are true he reaches a conclusion which proves his premises are false. The obvious self-contradiction nullifies the force of the argument.

It may be added that since skeptics assume the reliability of the mind in criticizing itself they contradict themselves. We must be on our guard, however, against an attitude quite prevalent among dogmatists of making a skeptic a man of straw and then knocking him down—dialectically speaking. Skepticism is often dismissed with the remark that it is self-contradictory. Of course if a skeptic were to maintain the self-contradictory proposition, "I am certain that nothing is certain," or if he doubted the existence of his own conscious states, or if he denied the principles upon which inference is based, it would be futile to argue with him. In that event he is outside the pale of rational discussion; he is a philosophical pariah. But such a skeptic is uncommon. The skeptic of to-day admits that he has convictions; he is ready to argue about them and in so doing to abide by the canons of logic. He only doubts their validity. He holds convictions to be merely subjective—their objectivity being a matter of doubt.[6]

---

[6] All epistemologies deal with skepticism. Consult in particular, Vance, *op. cit.*, chap. 2; Coffey, *op. cit.*, Vol. I, p. 153; Jeannière, *op. cit.*, p. 120; Montague, *op. cit.*, p. 172; Balfour, *Defense of Philosophic Doubt*.

CHAPTER IV

AUTHORITY, INNATISM, INTUITIONISM

It is manifestly impossible for us to attempt to trace each of our convictions back to its origin. Their vast number forbids that. We are aided in our endeavor, however, by the thought of various philosophers who have been engaged in a similar quest. All theories of knowledge must account for the genesis of knowledge and an analysis of the different attempts to solve this question will throw considerable light on the perplexities of the problem that confronts us. The history of philosophy evidences the fact that there are six outstanding theories regarding the source of our convictions. These are: (1) Innatism or apriorism, (2) Intuitionism, (3) Pragmatism, (4) Sensationalism, (5) Rationalism, pure and critical, (6) Moderate realism.

AUTHORITY

Before proceeding to a discussion of these theories the rôle which authority plays in the formation of our convictions must be noted. Introspection shows us that most of our convictions are derived from the testimony of our fellow men, past and present. A candid scrutiny of our certitudes would convince us that there are very few of them which are the result of our own reasoning. Life hurries us on—its demands are insistent. We have neither the time nor the intelligence to think things out for ourselves. We are forced by the pressure of life to accept most of the truths to which we give unquestioned assent on the authority of others. We

ELEMENTS OF EPISTEMOLOGY 37

are suggestible by nature; we have a natural inclination to give credence to the word of another unless we have positive reasons for doubting him. Hence it is to be expected that authority should loom so large in the formation of our certitudes.

It is apparent that authority cannot be an ultimate source of truth. If we trace a conviction to authority A, then either A got it from authority B, or he proved the truth to himself, i.e., he established the truth without recourse to an authority. The same is true of B. An infinite series of authorities is impossible. The series must end with some authority, and that authority must have acquired his conviction from the intrinsic evidence of the truth in question. In our search for the sources of our convictions authority may, therefore, be discarded; it is important but it is not ultimate.

Innatism

This theory as to the source of our convictions is so-called because it holds that we are born into the world with our convictions already formed. We are not conscious of these convictions in our infancy; they become actualized with the passing of the years. The process of learning whereby we seemingly acquire new truths and new convictions is in reality not a process of accretion but rather a process of explicitation or actualization of that which has been virtually present in our minds from the beginning. Plato (427-347 B.C.) was an innatist. With him "our birth was but a sleep and a forgetting" of the Ideas which we knew in a former period of our existence. The things we sense in this world do not engender knowledge in us except in the sense that they remind us of what we once knew. Leibniz (1646-1716) held that there could be no interaction between the monads which constitute the universe. It followed that the world could not act on the mind and rouse representations of itself in the mind. To account for knowledge he was forced to fall back on the doctrine of innate ideas. These ideas are not clear and distinct in the beginning. But gradually by virtue of the "preëstablished harmony" which rules the universe they acquire clarity and self-evidence.[1]

Rosmini (1797-1855) held that the idea of being was innate.[2]

CRITICISM: The theory of innatism finds no favor with modern thinkers. In fact it never had many adherents. It was not established on an empirical basis, i.e., experientially, as is evident from the nature of the theory. It cannot be proved that we have ideas at our birth. The various forms of innatism were integral parts of wider philosophical systems, and they arose from the context of those systems. The proponents of innatism were forced to adopt it because of the demands of their several systems. Since we are unconscious of the presence of ideas in our minds when we are born, the existence of the latter cannot be established, and hence this theory is a gratuitous assumption.

Secondly, it is an unnecessary assumption. Unless it can be demonstrated that some of our ideas cannot be accounted for by the knowledge-processes which function in our adolescent years such an assumption is unwarranted. We shall endeavor to prove in a later chapter that the combined functioning of our senses and our intellect can and does account for all our knowledge.[3]

Again, introspection shows us that our ideas even of suprasensible things is often accompanied by sense images.[4]

This points to the sense origin of our ideas. All our

---

[1] See his *La Monadologie*, passim.
[2] Descartes' doctrine of the *innatae ideae* was developed by some of his followers into a theory of innatism although he himself disclaimed innatism.
[3] See pp. 56, 195.
[4] See p. 57.

earliest ideas are of objects we sense; the very terms we use to express our most abstract ideas are drawn from sense experience—both of which considerations seem to indicate an intimate connection between percept and concept, a connection which any theory that maintains that we have ready-made concepts cannot explain.

It would appear, therefore, that the innatistic theory as to the source of our convictions must be rejected.

Intuitionism

The term "intuition" has diverse significations. It usually designates direct apprehension through sense perception. Sometimes, as in the present context, it means an immediate insight into reality through an intuitional faculty. Many of the finer spirits of philosophy have embraced intuitionism especially as regards the knowledge of God. They claim that the knowledge of God is best achieved through intuition, and not through the devious paths of discursive thought. Among those who held this view are Plotinus, Saint Theresa, St. John of the Cross, Master Eckhart, and the mystical school generally. We prescind here from this belief of the mystico-religious school, and confine our attention to that tendency in modern philosophy which maintains that knowledge of the universe gained through intuition is superior to that achieved through the intellect. The chief contemporary protagonist of this tendency of thought is the distinguished French philosopher and scientist, Henri Bergson.[5]

Bergson disparages the worth of rational thought because, in his opinion, the intellect in its endeavor to comprehend reality misrepresents and even falsifies the presentments of

[5] *Time and Free Will* (1910); *Matter and Energy* (1911); *Creative Evolution* (1911); *Introduction to Metaphysics* (1912); *Mind Energy* (1920).

reality. The intellect, since it acts in response to the need of man, is selective; it isolates parts of reality, it oversimplifies reality. And, while it purports to give an adequate description of reality, it really comprehends but a small portion of reality. It represents the universe as static, whereas in reality it is the opposite. It represents motion as a succession of points, whereas motion is a continuous flow. Similarly it erroneously represents the lapse of time as a succession of moments. The intellect is, as Bergson says, cinematographic. Just as the cinematograph takes a series of pictures of a parade, each of which represents the paraders as static, so does the intellect represent to the mind the continuous flux which is reality as a series of static states. Moreover, the intellect reads its notions of cause and substance into the constant flow of reality, whereas reality is neither cause nor substance as these are commonly understood. If we are to acquire an adequate knowledge of the universe we must rid ourselves of the prejudices resulting from our practical needs which is but another way of saying we must discard intellection. We must use our intuition instead of our reason because it is the former which alone can guarantee us a knowledge of the true nature of reality. What is intuition? "By intuition is meant the kind of *intellectual sympathy* by which one places oneself within an object in order to coincide with what is unique in it and consequently inexpressible." In intellectual knowledge "we move round the object," while through intuition "we enter into it." [6]

CRITICISM: The metaphorical expressions with which Bergson clothes his intuitionism are not to be taken literally. When we know the Atlantic Ocean we do not "enter into it." We do not literally "place" ourselves within the reign of the Roman emperors when we study that period of history. In fact the nature of knowledge seems to require that

[6] *Introduction to Metaphysics*, pp. 1, 6.

we never merge with a thing when we know it. The known object and the knower of that object are never identical; the polarity between them is a basic trait of all knowledge. Even when we apprehend our own experiences the process of apprehension whereby the experience is apprehended is never identified with the experience which is apprehended. The duality of subject and object in knowledge is a commonplace.

The strictures of Bergson against the intellect are ill-founded. This will appear in detail later. It may be said at this juncture, however, that if the intellect does not fabricate of itself the concepts of cause and substance, for example, but finds a basis for them in reality, then these concepts, while inadequate in as much as they do not express the full richness of reality, are true. The intellect does not impose these concepts on reality wrongfully—it finds them already existing in reality, and hence it can legitimately attribute them to reality.[7]

Are such things as causes and substances truly in reality, or are they, as Bergson maintains, sheer intellectual, and therefore inept constructs. Bergson says that when the intellect carves a chair or a book out of the flow of reality it does so because these objects are needed. It might just as well have carved out an elephant or a golf club, as it would have, if they were needed. But we know that it frequently happens that the intellect cannot carve out of reality the kind of objects it would have naturally chosen if it were left to itself. Reality cannot be treated thus arbitrarily. It imposes its laws on us; we must defer to it—it does not defer to us. Things are what they are and neither our volitions nor our thoughts can change them. This points to the fact that what we carve from the flux of reality are not arbitrary intellectual constructions, but that our conceptions

[7] See pp. 86, 201.

correspond to differentiations which exist in reality independently of our thinking of them.

Furthermore, it ill becomes a philosopher to disparage the validity of intellectual thought, for the intellect which he disparages is the tool which enables him to erect his philosophical system. When Bergson avers that the intellect cannot give us a true report of the universe, he makes an intellectual statement about the nature of the universe, i.e., the universe is not what the intellect reports it to be. What is Bergson's whole system but a construction of the intellect? The charm and lucidity of his works, their subtle dialectic, their argumentation, all bear eloquent testimony that he has utilized his highly developed intellect in the writing of these works. They are, moreover, addressed to our intellects with the avowed intention of establishing beyond the possibility of cavil that our intellects are not dependable. If these works are convincing, then Bergson's philosophy, which is highly intellectual as an attempt to understand it will prove, is a false philosophy. The closer he comes to proving his point, the more he discredits his own philosophy.

Intuition Not Infallible. None of our cognitional faculties are infallible means of knowledge. At least this seems to be the verdict of our introspection when we reflect on the causes and sources of our erroneous convictions. While we may acquire much truthful knowledge through intuition, the fact of the matter is that intuition is not an infallible source of knowledge, as we can readily see from an examination of our intuitional knowledge. Intuition is least liable to error in the practical affairs of our everyday lives. For example, we instinctively recognize friendship and enmity in others. But even in instances such as these we may be deceived, as we no doubt have been. When it is a question of highly abstract matters, such as the truth or falsity of metaphysical questions, instinct is a very uncertain guide to truth.

This is evidenced by the fact that the intuitions of different people lead them to adopt contradictory views on the same question.

It would seem to be more in conformity with the rational nature of man to accept intuition as a source of truth if and when its reports withstand the test of intellectual scrutiny. We have intellects and it is unreasonable to demand that we accept the pronouncements of any faculty unless those pronouncements survive intellectual analysis. We should not, as rational creatures, rely blindly upon intuition. The latter must subject itself to reason. Children trust in intuition to a greater extent than do adults; the uneducated are guided by it to a greater extent than are the educated. It may be said that, generally speaking, the more cultured and sophisticated the mind the less it trusts the validity of intuitional knowledge. And this is because mankind has found that while intuition may be the source of some convictions, it is necessary that intuitional convictions be validated by the intellect before an intellectual creature can give them assent.[8]

---

[8] See Russell, *Scientific Method in Philosophy*, p. 11; Hocking, *Types of Philosophy*, p. 175; Gunn, *Bergson and His Philosophy*; LeRoy, *A New Philosophy by Henri Bergson*; Lindsay, *The Philosophy of Bergson*; Stephen, *The Misuse of Mind*; Stewart, *A Critical Exposition of Bergson's Philosophy*.

CHAPTER V

PRAGMATISM

THE past few years have seen the rise, chiefly in the United States, of a new trend of thought which offers a different and distinctive answer to the question: What is the source of our certitudes? This school adopts the genetic approach in their solution of this question—and in their solution of philosophical questions in general. That is, they believe that if the genesis of knowledge is made our starting point in the study of knowledge, our conclusions will be more in accord with the results of modern psychology and logic; they will moreover avoid the endless and futile discussions which have marred the traditional epistemologies. The view of this school is called pragmatism. Pragmatists disclaim the belief that pragmatism is a definitely articulated system of philosophy; it is, they say, rather a philosophic attitude. However, they discuss various logical and metaphysical problems, as we shall see later. Here we shall consider the pragmatic doctrine on the source of knowledge.

Pragmatism may be traced to an article in the *Popular Science Monthly* of January, 1878, written by Charles S. Peirce. In this essay Peirce pleaded that the meaning of an idea can best be ascertained from the practical consequences of the idea in human conduct. Despite its novelty little or no attention was paid to this opinion until its revival by William James in 1898.[1]

---

[1] See James, *Pragmatism*, p. 46; this work and his *The Meaning of Truth* are devoted to James's version of pragmatism.

James maintained that the older psychology which held that knowledge results from reality being brought into contact with the mind through various isolated sensations is erroneous. The mind does not interpose connections between distinct and isolated sensations. For example, the view which avers that I am made aware of this book through the various sensations I have of it, and which also avers that my mind links these sensed mental impressions together when it enunciates a judgment about the book such as, "This is a book of quarto size about epistemology," is the exact reverse of the truth. Consciousness is not composed of isolated and distinct mental states—it is a continuum. It is a continuous whole in which the mind makes distinctions. The mind is one and active. It does not interpose connections between sensations. On the contrary, it makes distinctions in the continuous flow of experience. The essential work of the mind is to break up and separate the continuum of experience.

Furthermore the mind does not make these distinctions arbitrarily, but in response to the demands and exigencies of life. The interests and purposes of the conscious self determine the selective activity of the mind.[2]

We could not live in a world which was an indeterminate flux. Hence it is that we carve out of the continuum of our experience such things as chairs, tables, books, automobiles, etc. We need them and hence we desire them. Mental processes and action are ever linked together—we think that we may act and thus live.

Applying this practical or pragmatic attitude to the question of the genesis of knowledge, the pragmatist holds that knowledge is in the beginning a response of a living, mental being to its environment. Soon this mere awareness of an environment is replaced by the interest which the knower

[2] *Principles of Psychology*, Vol. I, p. 9.

acquires in his environment. The latter comes to have a meaning, i.e., it is to be seized or avoided, and the like. Gradually language gives names to things, and finally there emerges the stage of abstraction, judgment, and the other higher mental processes. In brief, knowledge is ultimately the experience of the reaction of a conscious being to its environment. In the light of the experience which it has acquired the mind can deal with new situations which arise; it can, relying on its funded experience, control and dominate its environment.

INSTRUMENTALISM

John Dewey has developed a system of thought which has much in common with pragmatism, to which he has given the name "instrumentalism." This designation emphasizes one of Dewey's leading tenets, viz., knowledge is an instrument to be used chiefly in the domination of our environment. Although the underlying motives of Dewey's instrumentalism are logical rather than biological, he views knowledge from the evolutionary point of view. The various functions of the mind have been evoked in response to the demands of the environment of man. They are adaptations to that environment. Our various ways of thinking have grown to be what they are because they have proved themselves useful in formulating our reactions to the world in which we live.[3]

Knowledge is thus primarily and fundamentally practical. It exists for the sake of action. It does not enter into the mind casually, neither does it drift in from the extramental world in ready-made impressions. It is, in the last analysis, the result of the interaction of a mind and its cosmic surroundings.

[3] See Dewey's *Reconstruction in Philosophy*, p. 87; see also his *Studies in Logical Theory; How We Think; Essays in Experimental Logic; Experience and Nature; The Quest of Certainty.*

Humanism

American pragmatism has its counterpart in English humanism. The leading exponent of humanism is F. C. S. Schiller. His philosophy is a gesture of revolt against the absolutistic idealism which dominates the English universities.[4]

Schiller is of the opinion that our emotions and volitions have a great deal to do with our convictions. Our interests determine not only the objects of our thoughts but our thoughts of those objects. This is true even of our perceptions—we mostly sense those things which have a bearing on our welfare. We therefore experience a world which is largely the result of our preferences and needs. Our world is "humanized" in as much as it is known through the medium of our human interests.

James, Dewey and Schiller all stress the practical aspect of knowledge; for them knowledge is not an end in itself; it exists because it tends to action and to practical results. There are minor divergences between them. Dewey shifts the emphasis to the environment as the factor controlling the interaction between ourselves and our world, while Schiller stresses the human factor as the dominating factor in the interaction. However as to the point under discussion, viz., the practicality of our convictions and the emergence of the latter from the above-mentioned interaction, they are at one.[5]

CRITICISM: Pragmatism has never enjoyed a wide prestige. It has found some favor in scientific circles but it has never

---

[4] For idealism see p. 119. Schiller has written: *Humanism; Studies in Humanism; Plato or Protagoras; Formal Logic;* "Axioms as Postulates," in *Personal Idealism.*

[5] Others affiliated with the pragmatic movement are Russell, Kallen, Bawden, Tufts, Moore, Baldwin and Boodin, in the United States; Simmel and Mach, in Germany; Milhaud, LeRoy, and Poincaré, in France; in Italy, Papini—in his earlier writings.

gained many adherents in the ranks of professional philosophers. Many serious objections have been brought against it. Some of these will be discussed later; here our examination of pragmatism will be confined to its teaching on the source and character of knowledge.

Pragmatism's Faulty Theory of Consciousness. This school, as has been indicated, regards experience as a continuous stream out of which the mind selects certain aspects because of their usefulness or aptitude for service. Thought is fundamentally selective. The mind is not necessitated by the presentation of experience to select this or that particular aspect. It is essentially free in the exercise of its preferences. But does introspection bear out this contention? When we examine the way in which our knowledge is formed, is it not apparent that our environment often forces knowledge upon us, in the sense that we feel ourselves under compulsion as to what we cognize? Is it not equally apparent that very frequently we are compelled to become aware of realities which are antagonistic to our needs, and which thwart our desires? If our knowledge is to be true must we not adjust our judgments about reality to the reality which we are judging? If the verdict of introspection is worthy of credence the basic note in the pragmatic doctrine of knowledge is not founded on fact.

Knowledge is not wholly practical. Granting that knowledge is the result of the interaction of a mind with its environment, the deduction that knowledge never transcends the sphere of the practical is illicit—it is an undue restriction of the scope of the cognitive interest. Knowledge, considered either phylogenetically or ontogenetically, may have emerged as a practical interest, but that is no warrant for the assertion that it must remain practical. Pragmatism stresses unduly the instrumental aspect of thinking. The falsity of its position is due to the fallacious assumption that a being can only function within the limits of the causes which brought it into being. Once a being has been realized it can develop new needs which go beyond the causes which produced it. Thought may have been practical at its inception but introspection tells us that it goes beyond its practical beginnings. When man begins to think he becomes a thinking being, and he is thereby released from the necessity of confining his thinking to facts of practical interest. "Human beings no longer have merely the need to live, they have also the need to know. Man began to think in order that he might eat; he has evolved to the point where he eats in order that he may think." [6]

Knowledge is scientific or contemplative as well as practical because the world is intelligible as well as plastic. We all feel within us the urge to know for the mere sake of knowing. Curiosity, a species of "divine discontent," impels us to acquire knowledge, much of which is utterly impractical. Thinking is a means to an end, but it can become an end in itself. The enjoyment which comes from knowledge is one of the values which enrich life for us, and hence contemplative thinking is not necessarily otiose. "Distinterested contemplation and enjoyment of the beauty, grandeur, meaning, and order of things for their own sake are for some human beings inherently worthful functions of consciousness."[7]

This summary discussion of the pragmatic doctrine on the nature of knowledge cannot be dismissed without mention of the deprecatory attitude of this school toward metaphysical reasoning, and toward speculative philosophy in

[6] Montague, *The Ways of Knowing*, p. 158. See chap. V of this work for a good discussion of this point.

[7] Leighton, *The Field of Philosophy*, p. 360; see also Royce, "The Eternal and the Practical," *Philosophical Review*, Vol. XIII.

general. Pragmatists inveigh against abstract speculation alleging that it is futile and barren. They maintain that philosophy should be put to work. It should descend from the clouds and become pedestrian. It should busy itself in the answering of those urgent social problems that are clamoring for solution. This is an attitude of mind that is found not only among those of a pragmatic bent—it is found also among scientists. Despite its widespread acceptance this view cannot be sustained.

The chief reason forbidding its acceptance is that it is too exclusive. Philosophy should be practical—but should it be confined to that realm alone? A more comprehensive and a truer view of the function of philosophy includes its speculative as well as its practical function. It is worthy of note that in establishing his view of the instrumental character of our thinking Dewey has created a speculative philosophy. He proves that thought should not be speculative by a speculation. The practical value of his speculation

> seems at best only the negative one of clearing away supposed mental obstacles to change and reconstruction, and since its own metaphysical peculiarities are far more obscure and doubt-provoking than the practical attitude for which they are intended to supply a foundation, they are liable to weaken, rather than increase the possible influence for good which philosophy may exert.[8]

It may be asserted that those who deny the validity of metaphysical and speculative thinking do so at the risk of self-contradiction, for their very assertion that metaphysical thinking is nugatory is itself metaphysical.

The pragmatic account of the origin of our convictions

---

[8] Rogers, *English and American Philosophy since 1800*, p. 393; see chap. VII of this work for a critique of pragmatism.

may or may not be true. That problem does not fall within the scope of epistemology. But when the pragmatist, arguing from his peculiar theory of the inception of knowledge, goes on to prove the essential practicality of knowledge, he is clearly at fault.

CHAPTER VI

SENSATIONALISM

THE views on the sources of our convictions enumerated above have never been widely received. There remain for examination the two schools of thought which both historically and to-day dominate the field as regards the answer to this mooted question, viz., sensationalism and rationalism. By far the greater number of philosophers are members of either of these schools. They both merit, therefore, a more detailed exposition and criticism than has been given to the preceding systems.

DEFINITION OF SENSATIONALISM

Sensationalism, or sensism as it is sometimes called, is the system of thought which holds that all knowledge originates in, and can be traced back to, elementary sensations. As a theory that attempts to account for the validity of knowledge, sensationalism is called empiricism. The latter maintains that those ideas alone are valid which can be verified by sense experience.[1]

As a doctrine on the nature of reality sensationalism merges with phenomenalism, which is the theory that nothing can exist except what appears to the senses. Phenomena

---

[1] When sensationalism attempts to account for the origin and growth of knowledge it is combined in modern philosophy with associationism, which describes the process whereby our sense data are built up into knowledge.

ELEMENTS OF EPISTEMOLOGY 53

alone are sensed and therefore they alone exist. There is nothing in the universe, whether spiritual or material, which underlies the phenomena presented to the senses. Positivism, like sensationalism, holds that the sensible alone can be known. In its negative aspect it signifies a system free from all speculative elements, while positively it stresses the limiting of philosophy to the data and methods of the natural sciences. It is absolutely opposed to the a priori, and to any form of metaphysical speculation.

History of Sensistic Theories

Sensism has claimed as adherents some of the most influential philosophers of the past and present. Francis Bacon, although not an empiricist himself, favored that standpoint and gave a stimulus to that movement in his *Novum Organum* (1620). Hobbes reduced all philosophy to a knowledge of phenomena and their material conditions. Locke developed this doctrine further, and Hume, building on Locke, held that the ideas which make up knowledge are nothing but faint images of impressions (or perceptions). Condillac originated a somewhat similar theory in France. He differed from the English school of empiricism in his denial of internal experience as a source of knowledge. Positivism took its rise from Comte (1798-1857). He taught that every science passes through three stages, the theological, the metaphysical, and the positivistic. The positive stage, which rejects the validity of metaphysical speculation, the existence of final causes, and the knowableness of the absolute, and confines itself to the study of experimental facts and their relations, represents the perfection of knowledge. The main arguments advanced by Comte are: Psychological analysis shows that all human knowledge can be ultimately reduced to sense experiences and empirical associations, and the argument based on the progress of the human mind from theological preoccupations through metaphysical speculation to the positive stage. Positivism is widespread among contemporary thinkers. Among its modern supporters may be mentioned: Spencer, Huxley, Lewes, Tyndall, Harrison, Congreve, Beesly, Bridges, and Allen, in England; Ribot and Durkheim, in France; Ferrari, Ardigo, and Morselli, in Italy; Laas, Riehl, and Avenarius, in Germany.

The popularity of the sensistic attitude to-day can be accounted for in part by the fact that Comte vested the sensistic theory with a philosophical dignity. But the hold which it has attained on the popular mind is due to another factor—the amazing triumphs of science. Our age has witnessed the vast strides which science has made in divining the secrets of nature and in bending her to its will. This has had an inevitable effect upon the thought of the lay thinker. He is under the spell of science and the scientific method. Science has put its stamp as ineradicably upon his mind as it has upon his civilization. It has become a cult. The method whereby it has achieved its wonders is empirical or experimental; its final test is sense experience. It uses reason in the formation of its theories but it will not give credence to any theory until its validity has been attested by the verdict of the senses. Confronted by the results which science has effected through the use of an empirical technic many have come to the view that if sense knowledge is not the only kind of knowledge, it at least gives us a satisfactory veridical test. It is productive of results—much more so than the thin theorizings of philosophers. This fact, it would seem, accounts in large measure for the tenacious hold of sensism in its various forms upon the popular mind, and the corresponding deprecatory attitude of the popular mind toward a metaphysical philosophy. The widespread appeal of sensism does not, however, exempt it from the critical examination of the philosopher. Like all other theories of knowledge it must justify its claim to truth.

The Cardinal Tenet of Sensism

All our convictions come from sense knowledge or sense experience. Our convictions, furthermore, retain their sensile character even when they have to do with abstract objects. Sensists deny that we have any source of knowledge that transcends the senses or that is non-sensuous. They are thus at variance with all species of rationalism—that theory which holds that besides sense perception we have a non-sensory source of our convictions, viz., the reason or rational insight, and that through the latter we can know more than sense perception reveals.

The Senses

The number and kinds of the senses is a matter of dispute. The disagreement of psychologists in this regard is largely due to the different bases of division they use, some basing their division on the specialization of the organ, others on the nature of the stimulus, and others again on the quality of the consciousness. For us the question of the number and kinds of the senses is of minor importance. Epistemology is concerned with the question of their rôle as a source of our convictions—and with their trustworthiness.

To-day no school of philosophers denies the existence of the senses. Neither is the fact that they are sources of knowledge questioned. As we shall see, a few thinkers of the past thought that some of our ideas derived from the reason without the functioning of the senses. But to-day the axiom that our knowledge originates in sense perception is generally admitted. Philosophers may and do differ as to the significance of sense perception but they do not deny the fact that the ultimate source of human knowledge is sensation.[2]

The fact that we gain knowledge from the functioning of the senses is proved by the functioning of the senses. We open our eyes and we see. If we close them we do not see. We touch an object and we have a sensation of resistance; when we cease to touch it the sensation of resistance is no longer experienced.

The theory of sensationalism is true in as much as it states that our knowledge begins with sense perception. But, as we have seen, this theory holds that our knowledge is sense-bound, that it never loses its essentially sensile character. It is this tenet of sensationalism that will be subjected to a critical examination. We shall test the sensistic theory (a) of the origin of concepts, (b) of the origin of necessary judgments.

NOMINALISM

Nominalism is the name given to the sensistic theory of the origin of our concepts or ideas. The term "nominalism" comes from the Latin *nomen* which means "name" or "term," and it is applied to this aspect of sensism because the latter grants that there is a general or universal term, but it insists that the term alone is universal. There are no universal mental correlates or universal concepts which correspond to these universal terms.[3]

---

[2] The distinction between sensation and perception arises from the subjective and objective aspects of an act of sentience. Sensation refers rather to the consciousness of awareness of what is sensed; it means the modification of the sensory apparatus regarded as a subjective state. Perception, on the other hand, refers rather to the objective aspect of the sentient act, i.e., the apprehension of external reality given in sensation.

[3] By universal concepts are meant the objects of thoughts designated by class names, or general terms, such as "book," "man," "chair," "desk." These latter are "universal" because they are attributable to all the members of their respective classes.

The so-called concepts are mere names, terms which serve as labels for collections of things or series of events. There is no suprasensible faculty of knowledge, and hence there can be no apprehension of thought-objects that is suprasensible. Nominalists use the terms "intellect," "conception," "abstraction," "generalization," and the like but they hold that between sense perception and intellectual conception there is no essential difference—they differ not in kind but in degree. Concepts are but refinements of percepts.[4]

Nominalists base their position chiefly on the fact that the presence of concepts in consciousness is often accompanied by, and associated with, the presence of sense data or images. Introspection tells us such is the case, and this fact gives a certain amount of plausibility to their position, which because of this association concludes that the concept is not essentially different from percepts or images but that it is reducible to them.[5]

We shall endeavor to prove that the concept is not the image—in opposition to their contention that the concept is the image. We believe that we have concepts *and* images—and for the following reasons.

Arguments against Nominalism. We have concepts in the strict sense of the term. We prove this by introspection which shows us that there is a difference between concepts and percepts, or images.

First argument. (1) Concepts represent the nature or essence of whatness of a thing, prescinding from all its individuating notes. The percept and the image do not represent the nature or essence, but only the external qualities of an object, such as its color and size. They represent an object

---

[4] See Mill, *Examination of Hamilton*, 2nd ed., pp. 321, 394.
[5] Introspection shows us that even when we are thinking of such abstractions as justice, idea, and virtue, along with the idea or concept, there is at the same time a picture, or a series of pictures, present in the imagination.

more or less concrete, with certain individuating characteristics, in a definite situation etc.

(2) The concept is universal, since it is capable of representing equally all members of a class. This is because it represents the essential characteristics, and these alone, of all the members of a class. For example, the concept "horse" is predicable of all horses, no matter what their size or kind or color may be. The image, whether it is distinct or obscure, is not universal; it can picture only one individual, of some particular kind and color. If we think "horse" and note the accompanying imagery we see at once that the concept is not to be identified with the imagery since the concept can be applied to all horses indiscriminately, while the image can be attributed only to a horse which it resembles.

(3) The concept is immutable and necessary; it cannot be otherwise than it is. If we add to it, or subtract any note from it, it no longer represents its object. The image, on the other hand, is unstable, contingent, and fluctuating.[6]

This can be verified by introspection. My concept of a man has the two notes of rationality and animality. If my concept is to be a concept of a man it must contain these two notes and these alone. If I add a new essential note, or if I take away either animality or rationality, I no longer have the concept of a man. In other words, my concept is unchangeable and fixed. But the same is not true of images. They change even in the same person as introspection shows. The same concept will be accompanied by varying imagery in the same person at different times.

(4) Concepts may be perfectly clear but the concomitant imagery may be extremely hazy. My concept of a million-sided figure is clear—I know what such a figure is. The same is true of my concepts of minute things; my concept of a cell that is one one-thousandth of an inch in diameter

---

[6] St. Thomas, *Summa,* q. 94, art. 1.

is perfectly clear. But is the accompanying imagery as clearly defined? What is the verdict of introspection? If the concept is clear and the image is hazy they cannot be identified.

Second argument. Appealing again to introspection I find that my concept is not a sense datum, but that it is a thought-object apprehended apart from all sensory characteristics. Granting that I am conscious of an image when I think "horse," "virtue," "triangle," it is not about these sensuous images that I enunciate the judgments, "The horse is an animal," "Virtue is good," "A triangle is a figure." I certainly am not speaking of "the (pictured) horse," "the (pictured) virtue," or "the (pictured) triangle." In making these judgments I mean "all horses," "all virtue," and "all triangles." The image, to repeat can only picture the individual, and if we had no concepts we could make no universal judgments.

Third argument. Nominalists admit that the name or term is universal, but they hold that there is no mental correlate which is really universal corresponding to it. But it would seem that the term can have no universal significance unless its mental correlate is universal, because language derives its significance from thought—not thought from language. The term itself, whether written or oral, is concrete. It is general or universal because it is the expression of an idea that is universal. If there is no concept of which it is the expression it is a mere concrete symbol of experience. Hence its universality is given to it by the concept for which it stands. The admission of nominalists that there are universal terms is thus an argument against their theory.[7]

Our position is strengthened by the results of psychological

---

[7] See Maher, *Psychology*, chaps. 11, 12; Mivart, *Groundwork of Science*, p. 10; Walker, *op. cit.*, p. 51; Coffey, *op. cit.*, Vol. I, p. 312; Moore, "The Process of Abstraction," University of California, *Publications in Psychology*, Vol. I, no. 2; *Image and Meaning in Memory and Perception, Psychological Monographs*, 1919, Vol. XXVII.

investigation. Psychologists have established two facts concerning the relation between image and thought: (1) that different persons differ considerably as regards the images that accompany their thought on one and the same objects; (2) that images vary in the same person. Hardly anyone experiences the same images on successive occasions when thinking of the same thing.

If our images were our concepts how could words be used as vehicles of thought? If our universal terms stand for varying and unstable images how could the same words convey the same meaning to different people? For example, the term "animal" may arouse fifty different images in fifty different people. Yet all understand the word in the same way—it has the same meaning for all fifty. It is clear that if the images were the thought there could not be this unanimity in understanding. As a matter of fact I know that when I make use of universal terms I do not manifest my images to others; I manifest my thoughts to them. I know this because they understand me.

Objections of Nominalists. First objection. This objection may be stated in the words of Berkeley.

> I can consider the hand, the eye, the nose, each by itself abstracted or separated from the rest of the body. But, whatever hand or eye I imagine, it must have some peculiar shape or colour. Likewise the idea of a man I frame to myself must be either of a white, or black, or a tawny, a straight or a crooked, a tall or a low, or a middle-aged man.[8]

This objection exhibits the fundamental weakness of the nominalist position—a confusion of image and concept. It is true that we cannot imagine an abstract object. This does not prove, however, that we cannot think an abstract concept. We cannot form an abstract or universal image. The correct inference from this fact is that the nominalist inventory of

[8] *Principles of Human Knowledge,* p. 142.

our mental acts is incomplete—they have overlooked the existence of concepts. When I think "man" I have a concept which, if realized in an individual, will be either a white or black or tawny man, but the concept represents neither color nor size, but only human nature. And this is evident from that fact that I can predicate the concept "man" of a being who is of any color or size, provided he has the essentials of man, i.e., provided he is a rational animal. Hence my concept of a man is not in itself a concept of a black man or a white man, or of any particular kind of a man; it is universal because it is a concept that can be applied to all men. But, as Berkeley says, we have no universal images. Therefore we have universal concepts.

Second objection. There is no difference between the concept and the image because the latter can be, and often is, as universal as the former. Images of things which are frequently sensed or imagined become blurred; they become less clear and less vivid. They lose their definiteness and gradually become generalized and generic, and in this state they serve as a mental equivalent for different things of the same kind.

Granting the existence of these generic images, a little reflection shows that this objection is another telling argument against nominalism. The image, we are told, becomes generic or blurred the more frequently we sense or imagine the object it represents. The reverse is true of the concept. If I had seen but one triangle my image of it would be definite and sharply defined, while my concept of it might not be clear and adequate. The more triangles I see the less clear and definite my image becomes, while my concept becomes more adequate and clearer. This proves that the generic image is not the concept.

Third objection. This objection is based on the existence of "type" or composite photographs. By superposition of negatives photographers can obtain the so-called "type" picture. In this way they give us pictures of historical personages reconstructed from likenesses on coins, monuments, and the like, as well as pictures of various types of people. It is claimed that something akin to this process takes place in the mental process wherein a generic image is evolved.

A composite or generic image is not universal. A type picture is the mean or average of the different photographs of which it is composed, and because it is an average it cannot be universal, since averages are concrete and particular. All averages are of the same nature and kind as the things of which they are the average. So, too, with the generic image. It is an average and as such partakes of the singularity and concreteness of the various images which enter into its composition. No matter how generic or hazy the image may be it lacks the essential characteristic of universality.[9]

The answer of nominalism to the question of the existence of concepts does too much violence to the facts revealed by introspection and hence it must be rejected. For those who maintain a sensistic theory of knowledge it is a logical position to sustain. Once the existence of a suprasensible faculty of knowledge is denied, nominalism follows. Nominalists have been ingenious in their attempts to reduce all knowledge to sense knowledge, but they have failed.

Sensism and Necessary Judgments

Associationism. A necessary judgment, as indicated above, is a judgment in which the nexus, or connection, between the subject and the predicate is independent of all conditions and hence universal.[10]

On no condition can a necessary judgment be other than

[9] See Stout, *Analytic Psychology*, Vol. II, p. 180.
[10] See p. 28.

ent as we do. The existence of necessary judgments is a fact—and like all other facts in the field of knowledge it must be explained by all theories of knowledge. When sensism attempts to explain the fact of necessary judgments it is called associationism.

The associationism of J. S. Mill (1806-1875). This theory is so called because it essays to explain the fact that we enunciate our necessary judgments under compulsion by an appeal to the laws of association of ideas. The mind in presence of any state tends to reproduce the like of that state in past experience. In our experience the subjects and predicates of our necessary judgments have always been found in conjunction. Every time, for example, we have experienced "two and two" we have experienced "four." This constant occurrence of both these ideas has generated in us an inevitable tendency to pronounce that "two and two are four." But this does not mean that this proposition is objectively true. As Mills says, "We should probably be able to conceive a round square . . . if it were not in our uniform experience at the moment when a thing begins to be round it ceases to be square. . . . We cannot conceive two and two as five, because an inseparable association compels us to conceive it as four."[11]

It may be that "in distant stellar regions" two and two are five.[12]

Hence the necessity and irresistibility of necessary judgments is purely subjective and psychological. These qualities of necessary judgments arise from acquired mental habits; they have no objective basis.

CRITICISM: Associationism has few adherents to-day and hence we need give only one argument against it. If it were

---

[11] *Examination of Sir William Hamilton's Philosophy*, 2nd. ed., pp. 68-69.
[12] *Logic*, b. 3, chap. 14, no. 4.

true that the necessity of our necessary judgments is the result of repeated associations then the sense of necessity would grow on us gradually, i.e., after repeated associations. But we know that we recognize the necessity of the nexus after one experience. For example, the first time I knew what two and two were, and what four was, I realized that two and two were necessarily four. Even if I added them up innumerable times since, the nexus between them to-day is no more necessary than it was after my first addition. I may never before have made the judgment "four and five are equal to six and three," but although I am making it for the first time I recognize it as a necessary judgment. I grasp its necessity by a single experiment. Hence Mill's theory is inadequate.[13]

Evolutionary associationism. Herbert Spencer (1820-1903) saw the inherent weakness of Mill's theory, namely that the experience of the individual is not, taken by itself, a sufficient explanation of the formation of mental associations strong enough to account for the necessity of our necessary judgments. He attempted to remedy that weakness by adding to the mental associations of the individual the force of heredity which transmits and solidifies these experiences through the ages. Our ancestors had certain experiences which left traces or modifications in their nervous systems. These latter are inherited by successive generations until finally they become necessary laws of thought. We must make certain judgments necessarily because they have become so strong with their passage through the years that to us, the heirs of the ages, they are axiomatic. The reason I necessarily affirm "two and two are four" is because my ancestors, prehistoric and historic, had this experience, and

[13] For other arguments against this theory consult Maher, *op. cit.*, pp. 284-286.

with the passage of time the belief that two and two are four has become so fixed that I cannot deny it. This theory, too, makes the necessity of these judgments wholly subjective.

CRITICISM: This theory, despite its ingenuity, cannot be proved. Any hypothesis as to the nature and growth of the concepts of the human race in prehistoric ages is outside the pale of discussion. It is manifestly impossible for us to know what the experiences of such ancestors were.

Again, it is clear that such judgments as "Thirty-nine and forty-two are eighty-one," and "All equilateral triangles are equiangular," are necessary, and it is equally clear that in the long ages before mathematics were studied—or known—they were not made. On Spencer's theory they would not be necessary since it is only recently, comparatively speaking, that men first made them. Hence Spencer, like Mill, fails in his endeavor to give a satisfactory explanation of the judgments in question.

Other objections might be given against sensism but the above criticisms are sufficient to prove that it does not offer us a satisfactory account of the origin of our convictions. Its positive doctrine, that all our knowledge of the universe originates in sensations, is true. But when it denies that our knowledge depends on the functioning of a suprasensible faculty it goes contrary to facts. It sins by excess because it stresses unduly the empirical element of our knowledge; it sins by defect in as much as it denies to reason its rightful place as a source of our convictions.

Important consequences follow from a rejection of sensism. Sensists deny that suprasensible reality can be envisaged by the human mind, as they are forced to do by the logic of their system. This sensistic tenet has been widely adopted and it will not be out of place to see whether the sensistic answer to the question, Can suprasensible realities be known? is grounded on fact or not.[14]

The Basic Axiom of Sensism. The basic axiom of sensistic theories of knowledge, i.e., the suprasensible cannot be known because it cannot be experienced, is put forward as an established, self-evident truth which needs no demonstration. But since this axiom marks the cleavage between sensistic and non-sensistic theories of knowledge it cannot be accepted without question. It seems to be obvious, first of all, that we cannot set limits to knowledge from an a priori standpoint. The only method to be followed in setting limits to knowledge is the a posteriori or experimental method. If we are to theorize about knowledge we must study knowledge. There may be limits to knowledge but these limits must be discovered through a scientific investigation of knowledge itself. The question, "What *can* we know?" cannot be answered until we have answered the question, "What *do* we know?" Any estimation of man's capacity for knowledge which omits what man *de facto* does know is erroneous. No theory of knowledge can afford to overlook actual knowledge. For if it is to be a theory of knowledge worthy the name it must be based on an examination of all knowledge. Whatever claims to be knowledge should, therefore, have its claim dispassionately examined. Its claim should not be summarily set aside because of any superficial generalization or arbitrary assumption as to what is and what is not knowledge. In brief, a theory of knowledge must be judged by its treatment of knowledge—knowledge must not be judged by the theory. Hence a mere assertion that experience is the only kind of knowledge will not satisfy the critical thinker. He will demand proof for

---

[14] The existence of such realities is not the point at issue. If such realities exist, the proof of their existence falls outside the scope of epistemology. We are concerned here simply with their knowability.

the assertion. He will insist that the question of the limits of knowledge cannot be solved a priori; he will insist that it is unscientific for the ultra-scientific positivist to settle this perplexing question by cutting the Gordian knot with a simple denial of the existence and worth of suprasensuous knowledge. Whoever adduces evidence in proof of the existence and knowability of the suprasensuous, or whoever attempts to substantiate the validity of metaphysical speculation has a right to be heard.[15]

What proof can be urged in favor of the axiom of sensism? It is not self-evident in view of the fact that intellectual knowledge seems to be knowledge. Whatever proof is advanced must be either of an a priori or an a posteriori nature. There is no a priori reason for this axiom since there is no evident identity between being and sensible being, i.e., the ideas of "being" and "sensible" do not mean the same thing. The statement that "real being is necessarily sensible or corporeal being" is not self-evident. It is not unconceivable that there is a species of being which is not sensible, since the ideas of being and sensible being are not inseparable. Furthermore the ideas of "being" and "sensible being" have not the same content. The note of "sensible" or "corporeal" adds a new attribute to being, an attribute which is not contained in the notion of being. Hence it is quite possible that there is an intelligibility which belongs to being as such, independently of the intelligibility which attaches to corporeal or sensible beings. There may be no suprasensible beings, but if such beings do exist they may not be beyond the competency of the intellect. The existence of such beings is not intrinsically impossible, and we seem to know them. So much for the a priori argument for the essential tenet of sensism.

A posteriori arguments for the axiom of sensism. What

[15] Consult, Mercier, *The Origins of Contemporary Psychology*, p. 284.

of the a posteriori arguments in support of the sensistic position? As to the fact that all knowledge is sensistic, and that is the vital point for us, the arguments attempting to prove that concepts can be reduced to percepts and images break down, as we have seen above. Their endeavors to show that all judgments are experimental are likewise inconclusive. As regards Comte's argument based on the three stages through which the mind has passed, the history of human thought shows that it is without foundation. It may be admitted that at different times the efforts of men's minds are marked by a tendency either toward religion or metaphysics or the experimental sciences. But we deny that any one of these tendencies excludes the others, either in the thought of the individual or in the thought of the race. Aristotle was a scientist and a metaphysician. Leibniz, Descartes, and Newton were believers in religion, and they were at the same time scientists and metaphysicians. Kant, Helmholtz, and Wundt did not cease to be scientists when they became metaphysicians, and Kant, at least, was a Christian. Science was cultivated to a greater extent in the Middle Ages than is commonly known, yet it was an age of faith and an age of philosophy. The metaphysics of German transcendentalism followed on an age given to science and it was in turn succeeded by another age of science. The truth would seem to be that these stages of thought can and do exist simultaneously with each other; they have so existed in some of the finest minds humanity has known. The march from theology through metaphysics to science has not been as orderly as Comte would have us believe. His argument, like his theory in general, is too a priori; it is not founded on fact.

There are, therefore, no valid a priori or a posteriori reasons advanced which prove the truth of the basic axiom of sensism. It is merely a groundless and an arbitrary assumption. It is more—it is an erroneous assumption, as will appear from the following considerations.

No sensistic theory can give a satisfactory explanation of the fact that there is an essential difference between our concepts and our images. If sensists are consistent they cannot account for those characteristics of the concept which mark it off definitely from images and percepts. If they do account for these characteristics they do so at the cost of consistency, for they implicitly admit the existence of the intellectual faculty which their theory denies. In point of fact, sensism, confronted by the evident difficulties of its view of conception, often surreptitiously introduces activities such as reflection, the power of transforming images, and the like. This is tantamount to admitting that powers other than the senses function in the genesis of our knowledge.

Sensism Is Self-refuting. If sensists insist that only the concrete and singular and sensible can be known it is suicidal for them to have a theory of knowledge since a theory is an abstraction and not a concrete thing. A theory cannot be sensed, and therefore on sensistic premises cannot be known. It follows that sensists cannot have a theory of knowledge. In their very denial of the existence of metaphysical problems they implicitly admit the existence of those problems since the fact that there are no metaphysical problems cannot be sensed. "Subjectivism and positivism refute themselves . . . the subjectivist cannot consistently apply his own theory . . . and still retain his subjectivism; nor can the positivist do any better. Neither can build his own particular philosophic house upon the sands of his own detailed doctrine." [16]

[16] Spaulding, *op. cit.*, p. 254.

CHAPTER VII

RATIONALISM, PURE AND CRITICAL

opposed Empiricism Sensationism

THE polarity of solutions found in the answering of most epistemological problems is present in the discussion of the present question. The historic and contemporary competitor of sensism, the competitor which is directly antithetic to sensism, is rationalism. In epistemology rationalism is a term of diverse signification. In general it means the theory that knowledge arises in whole or in part from the reason. In its extreme or pure form, rationalism is the name given to the theory that the content of philosophy is generated from certain fundamental concepts by deduction. It designates the doctrine that the one source of true knowledge is the reason; the dictates of reason have a higher authority than the reports of the senses.

PURE RATIONALISM

Pure rationalism has but a historic significance for the modern epistemologist. It took its rise from Descartes. His method was developed by Spinoza (1632-1677), Leibniz, and Wolff (1679-1754) in turn. Pure rationalism was formulated in detail by the latter. Descartes' mathematical bent explains his tendency toward rationalism. He endeavored to carry over into philosophy the methods used in geometrical proofs. As he himself says:

Those long chains of reasoning, quite simple and easy, which geometers are wont to employ in the accomplishment of their difficult demonstrations, led me to think that everything which might fall under the cognizance of the human mind might be connected together in the same manner, and that, provided only one should take care not to receive anything as true which was not so, and if one were always careful to preserve the order necessary for deducing one truth from another, there would be none so remote at which he might not at last arrive, nor so concealed which he might not discover.[1]

Geometry proceeds by deduction from axioms and postulates to the discovery of new truths; philosophy should follow the lead of geometry. It should advance by way of deduction from assured axioms and definitions to the establishment of new certitudes.

The content of Spinoza's philosophy was different from that of Descartes' system of thought, but the method he so rigorously applied in achieving his position was that advocated by Descartes. He not only developed his doctrines deductively but he even presented them in a mathematical manner; he begins with a definition of substance and from it he deduces his philosophy, which he presents in propositional form.[2]

Leibniz also followed the method advocated by Descartes. He advanced the idea of a universal logic which would be to philosophy what calculus is to physics. He, like Spinoza, stressed the a priori in the formation of knowledge and correspondingly deprecated the value of the empirical element in the knowledge process. Wolff, a mathematician like Descartes, followed closely in the footsteps of Leibniz; he presented the latter's philosophy in scholastic form.

CRITICISM: Rationalism in its extreme contravenes the facts regarding the origin of knowledge as revealed by introspection. If we reflect upon the origin of knowledge we are forced to admit that our knowledge of the universe is derived from sense knowledge. The validity of sense knowl-

---

[1] *Discours de la Méthode* (Torrey's trans.), part 1, par. 10.
[2] See his *Ethics*, 1, def. 3.

edge has not yet been proved, but the fact of sense knowledge, whatever be the value of its truth-claim, cannot be denied. The reason acquires its data from the material furnished by the senses. Concepts are devoid of content unless they derive their content from percepts. Reason needs the data of experience, since it has no experiential material of its own—except the consciousness of its own activities. Furthermore, it is the data of sense experience which are its contact with the universe it seeks to explain.

Even if it be granted that the reason has the mysterious power of generating knowledge of the universe without recourse to the data furnished to it by perception, what guarantee have we that such knowledge is valid? How can we be assured that this knowledge represents the universe validity? The history of rationalistic theories evidences the fact that their conclusions, since they are divorced from the empiric element in knowledge, are often at a far remove from the truth. Rationalistic theories may reach consistent and logical conclusions as to the nature of reality, but these conclusions are, as they have been, irrelevant to the facts. Truth cannot be created by the reason; it must be discovered, and the work of discovery is accomplished partly by the senses and partly by the reason. The history of science and philosophy bears out this contention. All attempts to deduce a theory of reality from abstract concepts and universal truths have failed—and they will continue to do so.

Pure rationalism is a corrective of sensationalism but it goes too far in the opposite direction. It overstresses the work of reason in the knowledge process, and it correspondingly underrates the value of the contribution of the senses. The radical defects of this theory were seen by Kant (1724-1804) and he broached a theory of critical rationalism which he believed would avoid both the defects of sensationalism and the defects of pure rationalism. It was this theory which preëmpted the place that pure rationalism had occupied in the philosophic scene.

CRITICAL RATIONALISM.[3] KANTIANISM

Kant's philosophy was essentially a revolt against the empiricistic theorizings of Hume. The latter, arguing from the typical sensistic premise that we can know only what we can sense, had come to the conclusion that our necessary convictions were merely subjective; they had no basis in the objective order. It was with the aim of refuting Hume that Kant in 1781 wrote his epoch-making *Critique of Pure Reason*. He believed that Hume had proved conclusively the impossibility of basing the validity of knowledge on experience alone. He was convinced that some of our universal and necessary judgments are expressions of valid knowledge, those namely of the physical and mathematical sciences. These judgments, he thought, contain knowledge, whatever knowledge may be. But since Hume had proved that these judgments were not necessary and universal he was confronted with the dilemma of accepting Hume's conclusions, which he did not want to do, or of constructing a new system which would save the necessity and universality, and therefore the objectivity of these judgments. He called these latter judgments "synthetic a priori" judgments, and his whole effort is to prove that they are possible. If he could establish their possibility he believed he would have justified the validity of the principles of mathematics and the sciences —and therefore of knowledge.[4]

---

[3] The significance of the term "critical" in the present connection must be noted. "Critical" is not opposed to "dogmatic"—as is usually the case. In the Kantian usage it means rather an attempt to discover the a priori forms of knowledge.

[4] Kant nowhere proves that universal and necessary judgments are valid; he assumes that they are. Cf. N. K. Smith, *Commentary on Kant's Crit. of P. R.*, p. xxvii; Lossky, *The Intuitive Basis of Realism*, Eng. trans., p. 107.

Theory of Necessary Judgments. An idea taken by itself does not constitute knowledge. In order to constitute knowledge an idea must be joined to another idea in a judgment. Knowledge is formulated in propositions. But while all knowledge is contained in propositions not every judgment contains knowledge. There are two kinds of judgments— analytic and synthetic. Analytic judgments analyze an idea but they add nothing to it; they do not increase our knowledge. They are mere tautologies. The predicate is contained within the comprehension of the subject, and hence these judgments are merely explicative, merely verbal repetitions. An example of an analytic judgment is: bodies are extended. On the contrary when I say, "The sun is shining," I join to the idea of sun a predicate which is not contained in the comprehension of the subject. Judgments of this kind, i.e., which add to the subject a note which was not contained in it, a note which enlarges, enriches, and extends knowledge, are synthetic.[5] But not every synthetic judgment expresses scientific knowledge. In order to do this a judgment must be true in all cases, i.e., it must tell us not only what is but what must be. The proposition, "This is a warm day," although synthetic, is accidental and contingent since sometimes it is not warm. Hence it is not scientific. But when we state a judgment that is true in all cases, it is necessary and scientific. Examples of such propositions are: heat expands; seven and five equal twelve; a straight line is the shortest distance between two points; everything that begins to exist must have a cause.

But by what right can I say such propositions as these are necessary and universal, or true in all cases? Experience does not reveal all instances to me. It may be that in instances I

---

[5] For the difference between the Kantian and scholastic definitions of these two kinds of judgments, see Coffey, *Logic,* Vol. I, p. 177; Joyce, *Logic,* p. 53.

have not experienced heat does not expand, that seven and five are not twelve. Kant, we must remember, thought Hume was correct in maintaining we could never get a universal from particular instances. Hence judgments which are a posteriori, i.e., posterior to and based on experience, cannot constitute scientific knowledge. Nevertheless they are universal and valid, and to save their universality he argues thus: these judgments are not analytic since they extend our knowledge; hence they are synthetic. They are universal and necessary; hence they are not a posteriori. They must, therefore, be a priori, which in Kantian terminology means prior to, or antecedent to, all experience.[6]

There must be an a priori element in them to give them their universality and necessity. What is this a priori element? It is a necessity-producing groove of thought, which is an innate mental endowment existing in the mind prior to, and as a necessary condition for, all mental experience. Hence the judgments which alone have scientific worth are synthetic-a priori judgments. The judgments of the physical sciences and mathematics are of this kind. They are the result of a union or synthesis of a purely mental and necessity-producing groove of thought with the contingent data of experience. The necessity and universality of these judgments is conferred by the mind.

A priori conditions of knowledge in sensibility. All ex-

[6] There has been much misunderstanding of the meaning of "a priori" in the Kantian philosophy. He himself says (*C. of P. R.*, Mueller's trans., 2nd ed., p. 715), "We shall . . . understand by knowledge a priori knowledge which is absolutely independent of all experience, and not of this or that experience only. Opposed to this is empirical knowledge, or such as is possible a posteriori only, that is by experience." Windelband, *History of Philosophy*, Eng. trans., p. 534, (footnote) says, "A priori is with Kant, not psychological, but a purely epistemological mark; it means not a chronological priority to experience, but a universality and necessity of validity in principles of reason which really transcends all experience, and is not capable of being proved by any experience (i.e., a logical not a chronological priority)." See also Prichard, *op. cit.*, chap. 1.

perimental knowledge is particular and contingent. But even in perception there are universal and necessary elements, namely time and space. The latter are universal and necessary because everything we perceive is in time and space; we cannot represent any sensible object to ourselves without locating it in some space and without placing it at some moment of time. We can imagine the destruction of all bodies in space and the cessation of all events in time but we cannot imagine the destruction of space and time. Again, if bodies are to exist they must exist in a space that already exists. The same may be said of events. They must take place in time which exists antecedently to them. Both time and space are therefore antecedent to whatever is and whatever occurs. In a word, things and events cannot be conceived independently of the space and time they occupy—but space and time must be thought of as independent of and prior to their occupants. Hence space and time are universal and necessary elements of perception, and they cannot, since Hume's arguments are irrefragable, come from experience. Whence do they come? The only alternative is that they are a priori elements anterior to all experience; they are faculties of perception. They are elements which perception does not perceive, but which the mind draws from its own nature. They exist in the percipient subject prior to all experience; in a word, they are a priori intuitions. The ordinary man thinks he perceives time and space, that they are objects of perception. But he cannot perceive them since they are innate forms in him. They are not objects of perception but modes of perceiving objects—which modes inhere in the subject. They are the colored spectacles we wear—they are the molds into which our perceptions run.[7]

A priori forms of the understanding. Just as the intuitive

[7] Weber, *History of Philosophy*, Eng. trans., p. 449.

ELEMENTS OF EPISTEMOLOGY

faculty perceives all things in time and space, so the understanding molds its judgments according to mental forms called categories. The synthetic judgments of science are necessary and universal, and since the necessity and universality cannot be experimental, they must come from the mind itself. This necessity-producing and universalizing factor of the understanding is twelvefold, i.e., there are twelve categories, each category corresponding to a form of judgment.

KINDS OF JUDGMENT	CATEGORIES
1. QUANTITY	
Universal	Unity
Particular	Plurality
Singular	Totality
2. QUALITY	
Affirmative	Reality
Negative	Negation
Infinite	Limitation
3. RELATION	
Categorical	Substantiality and Inherence
Hypothetical	Causality and Dependence
Disjunctive	Reciprocity (Active and Passive)
4. MODALITY	
Problematical	Possibility—Impossibility
Assertory	Existence—Non-existence
Apodeictic	Necessity—Contingency

The work of the categories in synthesizing and unifying the manifold of experience is somewhat akin to the functioning of the a priori forms of time and space. They are innate forms which the understanding does not find in, but which it imposes on, the phenomenal world. They are empty forms which must be filled by experience if we are to have knowledge; of themselves they do not extend our knowledge. Things-in-themselves do not have unity, plurality, etc.; these latter are categories which exist in the mind alone. For example, by the judgment, "All men are mortal," we mean that there is in the extra-subjective world a real race of men, all of whom have the attribute of mortality. Kant would say that we make this judgment because the four categories of totality, substantiality, reality, and existence have molded and shaped our experience into this judgment.

It is evident that human knowledge is an amalgam of two elements—the "form" due to the constitution of the mind, and the "matter" due to the action of the external object. We can, therefore, know only the phenomenon, the mental state resulting from both factors. To the noumenon, the thing-in-itself, we can never penetrate since it is only revealed to us as shaped by the a priori forms of the mind. Our minds are so made that we can know in this way, and in this way alone.[8]

We may illustrate the Kantian theory by the following figure. There is the world of the not-self and the world of the self. The latter has a definite structure akin to a prism— the a priori forms of intuition and the categories. Just as a light in passing through a prism is broken up into colored rays, so the world of the non-self appears to the self in various modes in accordance with the structure of the mind. The mind acts as a refracting medium through which the data of experience must pass, and we can only know reality after it has passed through the refracting medium.

---

[8] Note the contradiction of this view. Things-in-themselves are unknowable and yet they are known to be things-in-themselves (i.e., they exist and there are many of them), and at least some of them act causally on the ego to produce sensations, i.e., they are known to be causes. The thing-in-itself either is or is not the reality back of the phenomenon. If it is, then since we know something of it through its phenomenon, it is not unknowable. If it is not related in any way to the phenomenon it is wholly unknowable, and in that event the very idea of the thing-in-itself is devoid of content.

This is the "Copernican revolution" which Kant effected in philosophy. Beyond doubt it is a revolutionary theory of knowledge. Most thinkers hold that nature dictates her laws to the mind, that the mind must conform to nature. Kant reverses the process. He held that the structure of nature as known to us is a product of the mind. In his theory it is not nature which dictates her laws to the mind but the mind which imposes her laws on nature.[9]

CRITICISM: We shall not attempt to criticize the Kantian system as a whole. We shall confine our critical examination to that part of his system which has to do with his endeavor to establish critical rationalism.

The fallacy of Kant's arguments in proving the subjectivity of time and space. It may be admitted that we cannot imagine bodies and events as existing outside space and time respectively. But does the subjectivity of space and time follow from this fact? Might it not be said that our inability to imagine them as stated is due to the fact that time and space are necessary and universal preconditions for beings and events in the objective order? Any genus is logically prior to its species. We cannot imagine a species without its genus, but we can imagine a genus without its species. We cannot think of a "brown book" without thinking of "book," but we can think of a "book" without thinking of "brown." This proves only that a genus is prior to and implied by its species—not that a genus is more subjective than its species. Besides there is something else which conditions all our thought and from which we cannot escape in thinking, and that is the

---

[9] It must not be forgotten that the whole Kantian system rests on a supposition he took from Hume. "The fundamental presupposition upon which Kant's argument rests—a presupposition never investigated but always assumed—is that universality and necessity cannot be reached by any process that is empirical in nature." Smith, *op. cit.*, p. xxxiii.

notion of being. If Kant were consistent he would have made it subjective as well as time and space—but he held that it was objective. In brief, the fact that we are unable to think of reality without time and space is no proof that they are exclusively subjective. The more natural explanation would seem to be that they are more fundamental objectively than the objects which they condition.

Granting that the truths of the sciences and mathematics are necessary—something which Kant never proved—does it follow inevitably that the necessary character of knowledge is the result of the functioning of a necessity-conferring mental mechanism? Can he argue that because seven and five are twelve, the necessity of this judgment is conferred by the mind? It may be held that the necessity which characterizes such judgments comes from the subject-matter of the judgment, and not from the mind, as we shall see. The characteristics of the subject-matter of a judgment should be explained by the characteristics of the subject-matter, and not by an irrelevant appeal to the nature of the mind. The reason why we judge seven and five are twelve is because in the objective order seven and five are necessarily twelve, and the necessity which is objective forces the mind to make this judgment necessarily. Kant's treatment of the question is faulty because he admitted the truth of Hume's position, and he thought his own solution was the only way out of the difficulty into which he was impelled. He overlooked another solution of the question which seems more reasonable.[10]

Kant did not prove this point. He set out to establish the objective necessity of our necessary convictions but he made their necessity only psychological and subjective. We must be on our guard when he uses the words "object" and "objective." We have seen above what we mean by these terms.

[10] See p. 86.

In the Kantian system, however, they have an entirely different signification. By the term "object" he cannot mean something distinct from the knower since, on his theory, we can know only the phenomenon which is not at all the extramental thing known as it is in itself, but that thing as molded by the forms of the mind. It is clear that the objectivity of these judgments is intramental; they are not objective in the ordinary sense of that term.

As to their necessity—the individual man is just as contingent as the world which he experiences. His mental makeup can explain why seven and five must equal twelve to his mind and to all minds similar to his. But this does not prove that a mind must be so constituted and cannot be constituted otherwise, viz., so that it cannot judge that seven and five are eleven. We have no assurance that our minds will always remain as they are. If their constitution were changed then seven and five might necessarily equal eleven—on the Kantian theory. This possibility destroys utterly the universality and necessity which Kant thinks he has vindicated for these propositions.[11]

In other words, a priori forms do account for a psychological necessity but they do not account for the necessity which we see is characteristic of these judgments. We are forced to judge that seven and five are equal to twelve not only for us and for minds like ours, but for all conceivable minds. We know this is so because seven and five *are* twelve, and this fact is the reason why all minds must think them thus and not otherwise. Despite the use of the word "objective" then, Kant proves these judgments have only a psychological necessity, which is not the point he set out to prove.

Kant's theory does not square with the facts revealed by introspection. What does introspection tell us of the way in

[11] See Russell, *Problems of Philosophy*, p. 134.

which we form our universal and necessary judgments? Does it reveal our minds as acting under the influence of blind, irresistible forms, or does it reveal them as forming these judgments under the influence of motives of which we are conscious? Do we form these judgments blindly or do we know why we do so? Introspection informs us that we are conscious not only of judging but also of the reasons or motives why we judge as we do. We are conscious that the nexus between the subject and predicate of a necessity judgment is affirmed not because we wish to affirm it, nor because we do it without motives, but because we see that the judgment must be affirmed (or denied if it is a negative judgment). We attribute the predicate to the subject because we see it belongs to the subject. We join the one to the other because the nexus is objectively existing and patently manifest to us.

On Kant's theory as soon as we were conscious of two concepts the understanding would form the judgment immediately and necessarily. But such is not the case. It often happens that the understanding is forced to refrain from judging, it often suspends judgment, even if it is conscious of two concepts. It may remain in a state of doubt or opinion. Why does it act thus? Because, introspection tells us, it does not see the nexus between the subject and the predicate; the nexus is not clear and evident to it. Once however the nexus becomes clear and evident, then and only then, does it affirm the predicate of the subject. Hence the reason why we judge, why we affirm the predicate of the subject, is not mental or subjective, but objective. For example, I may be aware of the two concepts, "23 plus 89 plus 46" and "158." I do not immediately affirm equality between them. Should I be asked if they are equal my first answer would be that I did not know—I doubt it. Then after a hasty addition I would be of the opinion that they were equal. After I had verified my first result I would be certain they were equal. On Kant's theory the category of equality would make me form the judgment without hesitation. Mercier says of this defect in Kant's thought,

> If the assent of my intellect were determined not by the manifestation of truth but by the constitution of the mind independently of the manifestation of objective truth, this succession of states (doubt, opinion, certitude) would be inexplicable. . . . That the same matter and the same category could produce now doubt, and again certitude is simply unintelligible (on the Kantian theory).[12]

It may be objected that it is illegitimate to test Kant's theory empirically, i.e., by introspection, since he himself says that we are unconscious of these forms in the mind, and hence introspection could never reveal to us the fact that they are part of our mental machinery. We reply that it is true that Kant vindicates the existence of the forms only on the supposition that they are the sole means of explaining our necessary judgments; it is true that Kant proves the existence of the forms deductively. But we believe that even if a theory is not based on facts of consciousness it should not in any event contradict the facts of consciousness, and this Kant's theory does. We are within our rights in attempting to square his theory with the results of introspection, and if it is found wanting we should reject it.

Kant's theory is self-contradictory. It is a legitimate procedure to test any theory by its own conclusions; a self-contradictory cannot stand. Kant maintained of course that the conclusions of his *Critique of Pure Reason* were correct—that this book gives us a knowledge of things as they are, that it represents to us the real state of affairs. But, as we

[12] *Crit. Gener.*, p. 256.

have seen, on his own theory we can never have such a knowledge. He appears to have thought that the conclusions of his *Critique* were *sui generis,* that they gave us a real insight into the a priori conditions of knowledge. And yet in this very *Critique* he proves that we cannot know things as they really are. Again, he seems to have believed that pure reason can, without experience, form true knowledge about the a priori conditions of knowledge. But he cannot, on his own theory, examine the nature or structure of the faculty of pure reason, since we have no experience of it, and for him the unexperienced is, and must be, unknown. In other words, granting that there can be no knowledge of anything we cannot experience, then we can never know the forms of the mind since we have no empirical knowledge of them. Hence, if they exist, they must remain unknown and unknowable.

Kant's solution of the problem of the origin of our convictions is not convincing. Waiving the criticism which might be directed against the logic of his attempts to establish the truth of his doctrine it cannot be gainsaid that the average man—and the average philosopher—will not accept the results of Kant's dialectic, i.e., that the mind in a very real sense recreates nature. If we recreate our world how explain the fact that we are subject to the laws of our world? It seems that we stress the obvious when we aver that the exact contrary of the Kantian position is true, viz., the world imposes its laws and conditions on us.

The Kantian position must, then, be rejected as untenable. It is a corrective of the extravagant claims of sensationalism. But it grants too much importance to the rôle played by the reason in the formation of knowledge, and it correspondingly restricts unduly the rôle played by the objective element of knowledge. The rationality and order of our knowledge of the universe does not, as we shall endeavor to prove, derive from the mind, but from the universe itself. We discover unity and order in the cosmos—we do not impose unity and order on the cosmos.[13]

[13] Neither an adequate exposé nor an adequate criticism of the Kantian system has been attempted. The Kantian bibliography is extensive and there is no difficulty in finding abundant criticism of this system. Coffey's *Epistemology* contains a thorough criticism. Prichard can also be consulted with profit. See Thilly, *History of Philosophy*, p. 395, for a bibliography.

CHAPTER VIII

MODERATE REALISM

THE position of moderate realism is midway between the two extremes of sensationalism and pure or critical rationalism.[1] With sensationalism it is committed to the view that our knowledge has its origin in sensations. With rationalism it holds that reason coöperates with the senses in the formation of our knowledge. It repudiates the claims of pure and critical rationalism of the sovereignty of the reason. Its own tenets as to the function of the reason in the knowledge-process will be unfolded as the theory is explained.

DISTINCTION BETWEEN THE SENSES AND THE REASON

The arguments given above against nominalism not only prove that nominalism is an untenable theory—they also prove that we have the power of generating concepts which are non-sensuous in character. Our minds must have, therefore, a suprasensuous faculty, the reason or intellect.

Introspection clearly evidences the distinction between our higher and lower cognitional powers. Through the senses we become aware of particular things. For example, through the sense of sight I see this or that particular object, possessing a certain size, shape, and color, existing in this place at this time. If we touch an object, the resistance we encounter

---

[1] The nature of this position would perhaps be better understood in the light of what has been said of other systems if it were called "empirical rationalism." However it is usually styled "moderate realism" in scholastic treatises—hence the present usage. However it must not be confused with "epistemological realism" which will be discussed later.

is this resistance, and if we strike it we hear this sound. Whenever we sense a reality, it is always endowed with individuality—it always has specific individuating notes. But reflection tells us that we have another kind of knowledge which differs widely from sense knowledge. It is not a knowledge of the particular and concrete, but of the general and abstract. I can, for example, think of a book which is totally different from this book I now sense, and which has none of its individuating characteristics. This new thought is no longer bound up with this particular book. It is applicable, as I can see by reflection, to any number of individual books. Its object is not a particular object but a universal object. Furthermore my senses do not tell me what things are; they do not apprehend the essence or whatness of things. But I seemingly do know what things are; I know not only the qualities of things but I also know what things are in themselves; I know their natures. Thus my senses alone do not tell me this is a book. They report color, size, shape, etc., but I *know* it is a book, proving thereby that I have a kind of knowledge which is not sense knowledge.

Again, I know what is meant by such notions as justice, hope, casuality, knowledge, none of which I can sense. None of these can be perceived through a sense organ, yet I can and do know them. Moreover, the senses have not the power of reflection. They cannot make their data the objects of their own examination. But the power of reflection is a fact, and this points also to a difference between sense knowledge and a higher kind of knowledge. Then there are our judicial and ratiocinative powers. These cannot be allocated in the senses. From a comparison of the conceptual, judicial, and ratiocinative aptitudes of the intellect with the functioning of the senses we see that there is a radical difference between the senses and the intellect.

But while we differentiate the one from the other, and

while we see they are irreducible to each other, we must not think that though distinct they are separate. Intellect and sense do not function separately and apart from each other. In actual concrete experience we cannot divorce the operation of the lower faculty from that of the higher. In our adult experience the sensuous and intellectual elements are closely interwoven. A sensation is hardly, if ever, given without an accompanying intellection. Continuity and solidarity are always present between them. So closely are they interwoven that it is often difficult to discriminate between the purely sensory elements in our knowledge and those which are the result of higher factors. We must not forget that the knowledge-process is complicated, and that sensation, perception, retention and reproduction, conception, judgment, and reasoning, all intermingle with one another, and that all have an integral part in the process of cognition.[2]

The existence of rational concepts has been established. The formation of concepts depends on and begins with sense knowledge, but it is completed by the intellect. The process whereby concepts emerge from percepts demands an exposition.

The Origin of Concepts. Since our concepts are not a priori (or prior to sense experience) and since introspection shows us that in our judgments we identify these concepts with the data of sense, the intellect must apprehend them in some way in the data of sense.[3] There is no other explanation. The intellect gets all its data or objects in and through sense perception—and self-consciousness. This does not mean that the intellect can conceive only what the senses

---

[2] For the distinction between the senses and the intellect see St. Thomas, *De Anima,* 111, lect. 8; *Contra Gentiles,* II, 66; Maher, *op. cit.,* p. 230.

[3] For the view that our concepts are a priori see p. 38. We are constantly making judgments in which we identify the data of sense with our concepts, e.g., "This is a book."

perceive, i.e., only the physical or material. This is the sensistic interpretation of this principle. The principle means that while the intellect gets its data from sense perception it nevertheless has the power of apprehending modes of being which transcend sense perception. For example, it can form such concepts as "being," "quality," "change," "thought," none of which objects can be the objects of the senses. Again, the intellect can reflect on its own activities and form concepts such as "intellect," "cognition," which are concepts of realities unperceivable by the senses. Our theory of moderate realism, therefore, which holds that the thought-objects of the intellect are somehow apprehended in the data of sense is not sensistic.

The theory of abstraction. Since the thought-objects of the intellect are apprehended in sense data, the obvious question arises: How is the concept derived from the percept—or sense data? How can we bridge the gap between sense knowledge and intellectual knowledge? The answer is: by the process of abstraction. An extramental object produces an impression on one or more of the senses. Through this impression the mind becomes cognizant of a concrete object. This impression evokes the activity of the intellect. In every object there are certain qualities or attributes which may or may not belong to the object without any substantial or essential difference being made in the nature of the object; e.g., the height, weight, and clothing of any individual may all be different from what they are and he would still be a man. There are other attributes, however, the absence of which would destroy the character of the object and cause it to be other than it is. If we did away with either the rationality or the animality of a man he would no longer be a man. The functioning of the intellect at this juncture is abstractive. Abstraction is the concentration of the intellect on these latter elements to the exclusion of the former. It is the withdrawal of the attention of the mind from what is accidental and the fixing of it on the essential. It is the act whereby the intellect abstracts or selects from an object that portion which is essential and neglects the rest. The result of this abstraction is the concept which expresses in the abstract the essence of the object. The concept is not the representation of a single, particular object; it is universal and abstract because, as we shall see, it is capable of being realized in an indefinite number of objects. In a word, the intellect *con*ceives what the senses *per*ceive but in a different way.

The term "abstraction" as descriptive of the conception process has given rise to much misunderstanding. Some have understood it as connoting the taking away of something from the concrete object. Such a view is a travesty on the nature of abstraction. The essence or nature which is said to be abstracted is an attribute of the object and it never ceases to be such. Abstraction is a purely mental process. It does not take away the physical essence of the object. Just as the eye can see an object without assimilating any of the physical properties of that object, so does the intellect represent to itself the object without changing in any way its physical reality. Abstraction does not change the nature of the object but rather the nature of our awareness of the object. In brief, abstraction simply means the representation of the essence of an object in the intellect.

The Universality of Concepts. The fact that concepts are devoid of the individuating characteristics which are always found in sensed objects has two implications.

(1) The thought-object considered in itself is neither universal nor particular.[4]

As James says:

---

[4] St. Thomas, *De Ente et Essentia,* c. 4; Calkins, *Introduction to Psychology,* p. 231.

The conception of an abstract quality is, taken by itself, neither universal nor particular. If I abstract white from the rest of a wintry landscape this morning, it is a perfectly definite conception, a self-identical quality which I may mean again; but as I have not yet individualized it by expressly meaning to restrict it to this particular snow, nor thought of the possibility of other things to which it may be applicable, it is so far but a floating adjective.[5]

The concept considered in this abstract condition is said to be the direct or potential universal, and as such it is fundamentally real, i.e., its basis is in the object independently of the work of the mind. We are warranted in claiming objectivity for the direct or potential universal since the mind finds the content of the concept in the object. The mind does not create the content of the universal by its own activity but it discovers the content objectively existing.

(2) After the direct universal has been generated the intellect sees that the thought-object is not only in this object and predicable of it, but that it is capable of indefinite repeated realizations in an indefinite number of other similar objects. It thus formally universalizes the concept. When by reflection a concept is seen to be universally predicable of all the objects of a class it is said to be a formal or reflex universal. Thus at first one forms the concept of man as a rational animal. This is a direct universal. By an act of reflection the concept "rational animal" is seen to be predicable of all men, past, present, and future—it is formally universalized.[6]

The universalizing is the work of the intellect. Hence universals, as universal, exist in the mind alone. The concept of the nature or essence which is universalized has its basis in the object of sense, but the universality and abstractness

[5] *Psychology,* Vol. I, p. 473.
[6] St. Thomas, *Summa,* I, q. 39, art. 3; *De Anima,* lib. 2; *Summa,* I, q. 85, art. 2, ad 2.

which characterize the concept are the work of, and are in, the intellect. There are universal thought-objects but no universal objects. Whatever is real, i.e., in the real or objective order, is individual. But individual things, while they do not constitute one reality, have similar natures. Because of this the intellect can apprehend this similarity of nature and form a concept, which it may universalize, and which is predicable of the various different but similar individuals. This predication of the same attribute to different individuals does not imply that they are the same reality. They are distinct and separate individuals, but because of their similarity of nature the same essence can be predicted of them. Similarity is not a real identity—it is a mental identity.

Extreme realism. The view that there are no universal objects is disputed by the theory known as extreme realism. This theory agrees with moderate realism as regards the existence of concepts. But while the latter theory holds that only our concepts are universal, and that individual things alone exist in the extramental order, this theory maintains that there are both universal concepts in the mind and universal realities in nature. It holds that the world of thought is paralleled by the world of reality in as much as extramental objects are clothed with the same character of universality that we discover in the concept.

Platonic realism. For Plato the objects of our concepts were the Ideas. These are not constructs of human thought, but are mind-independent realities which the mind knows. They are not in the mind; they have their being above and beyond this world of sense in the world of Ideas. To every concept we can have there corresponds a reality—which is abstract and universal—an Idea, and it is this latter which our concept represents to us.

Empiric realism. This is the name given to the system of William of Champeaux (1070-1120). He, like Plato, held that the universal as such existed extramentally, but he maintained in contradistinction to Plato that these universal objects exist in the individual things of sense experience. The generic universal is really one, unmultiplied, self-identical essence shared by all its subordinate species, while the specific universal is one reality shared by all the individuals of the species. Individuals differ not really and substantially but only by the accidents which individuate the common essence.

CRITICISM: The best argument against extreme realism is the exposition of moderate realism given above. That theory accounts for the existence of concepts; it maintains that while our concepts are abstract and universal only individual things exist in the objective order. It is therefore in full accord with experience. It makes unnecessary the postulating of universal realities to which our concepts correspond. As regards Plato's theory of universals, it is but a unit in his system as a whole—hence it suffers the fate of that system. To-day Platonism has been discarded as too unreal and artificial, as a detailed study would show.

If it is held that an individual object is a participation of an Idea (Plato) or that it is a part of a universal substance (William of Champeaux), then all our singular judgments would be invalidated. "John is a man" would mean to the extreme realist that "John is a manifestation or a participation of the transcendent reality 'man,'" or that "John is a part of the single reality called humanity." A little reflection tells us that when we make this judgment we mean neither of these. Hence this theory must be rejected as doing violence to common sense.

JUDGMENT

It is clear that the senses and the intellect coöperate in the production of our concepts. But what of our judgments? Are they the result of a reason, such as the rationalistic school avers, which operates mechanically and according to its own constitution? Has reason the power of transmuting the data presented to it by the senses? Does it arrange these data according to its own categories? Does the reason unify and harmonize these data according to its own laws, or is it guided by the objective order? Are our judgments grounded on the objective order or are they grounded on the subjective order? The answer of moderate realism, briefly stated, is that the ground of the nexus between the subjects and predicates of our judgments lies in the subjects and predicates themselves, whether they be percepts or concepts. We join the predicates to the subjects of our judgments (or negate them of subjects of negative judgments) because we see they must be joined (or negated). The nexus reveals itself to our minds when we scrutinize the subjects and predicates, and when we become aware of it we make the judgment. In support of this position three arguments may be adduced. In these arguments we appeal to the only court we have, namely introspection. We must not, like the others who have pondered this problem, solve it in such a way that it will fit in with a preconceived theory of knowledge.

The problem cannot be solved a priori; it must be solved in accordance with the facts made known by reflection.

The Objectivity of Our Judgments. First proof. If I scrutinize the mental processes which take place when I form a judgment, I observe the following: I identify the predicate with the subject only after I have compared the two and have seen that they are identical. It is this identity which compels me to affirm the identity. I do not identify the predicate with the subject until I see that they necessarily involve the identification, but when I see that they do involve it, then and only then do I affirm it. In case of abstract judgments in order that I may see whether the two concepts involve the identity I analyze each in its simplest elements. Thus in the judgment, "Two and two are four," I analyze the subject into its units—one plus one plus one plus one. I do the same with the predicate, and I have one plus one plus one plus one. It is then that I see they are identical. The identity becomes clear by analysis, and because, and when, it manifests itself to me, I affirm it.

The same is true as regards the processes I go through in enunciating concrete judgments. I perceive this book through the media of sight and touch. I analyze the data presented to me, and it becomes apparent to me that it is a book about epistemology. I make the judgment, "This is a book about epistemology"; I make the judgment because the nexus between "this" and "a book about epistemology" is clear and evident to me.

The nexus is not, therefore, something subjective. Neither do I affirm it blindly. I examine the motive for my assent, and I know why I make the judgment as I do. I say, "Two and two are four" because I see two and two *are* four, and I say, "This is a book about epistemology" because I see it *is* such a book. Briefly, the nexus is objective; it is not something which I make but it is something which I discover. And when I discover it and it is evident to me I make my judgment in conformity with it.

Second proof. This argument is based on the different states of mind which may exist in the presence of the same two concepts. It is an undeniable fact that the mind in the presence of the same two concepts often passes through the successive stages of doubt, opinion, and certitude, as we have seen above. We can take as an example any mediate necessary judgment of the ideal order such as, "The square inscribed on the hypotenuse of a right-angled triangle is equal to the sum of the squares inscribed on the other two sides." When first confronted with this proposition I do not know whether it is true or not—I doubt it. I then analyze the terms of the proposition, and with the aid of inference I come to the conclusion that it is probably true—I pass from doubt to opinion. I reëxamine my reasoning, I find my opinion is true and then I become certain. This proves that if the nexus is not evident I endeavor to see if it exists, and if I am successful, if I discover it, I assent to it. I do not make the nexus; it is something which manifests itself to me as already existing; it is objective.[7]

Third proof. This argument is based on the difference between conscious states resulting from sensibility and those which are the result of the intellectual act of judging. Experience shows me that the senses necessarily report things as they appear, even if the appearance be different from the reality. A straight stick partly immersed in water appears bent. The senses cannot of themselves distinguish between the appearance and the reality. The intellect can, by taking account of the conditions under which the object was sensed —in this case the vision of the stick through the media of air and water—refrain from identifying the appearance with the reality. It can, to use the above example, refuse to pronounce that the stick is bent even though it appears bent. This goes to show that the mere presence of two thought-objects in the mind does not force the mind to make a judgment. It makes a judgment only when the nexus between the thought-objects is evident. Introspection tells us further that even after we have made a judgment the intellect can retract its assent and go over the motives of assent until the nexus becomes clear and compels its assent.[8]

CONCLUSION OF THE FIRST PART

The answer to the first of the two main questions has been

[7] This argument also holds true of concrete judgments, as introspection shows.
[8] See Coffey, *Epistemology,* Vol. I, p. 232.

achieved. Human knowledge derives ultimately from two sources—the senses and the intellect. It is an amalgam of two elements, the sensuous and the intellectual. As said above, the senses and the intellect are different sources of knowledge but they do not function separately. The senses furnish us the isolated data; the intellect interprets these data and gives them a coherence and solidarity. The senses furnish the food which the intellect digests. The intellect is guided in its functioning by the data presented to it. It does not pronounce upon them arbitrarily, nor does it read into them meanings and values which are foreign to them. Its conceptions, judgments and reasonings are, or should be, conditioned by the reality known. It does not invent meanings and values—it discovers them objectively existing.

CHAPTER IX

THE TRUTH OF KNOWLEDGE. REALISM

THE second of the problems which confronts the espistemologist remains to be solved. It is the problem of the validity of knowledge. We have accounted for the origin of knowledge but we have not yet proved that knowledge is, or can be, true. The problem of the validity of knowledge is easily understood. There is, as has been indicated, an evident gap between our knowledge and the objects of our knowledge. One is not the other. Knowledge is intramental and psychic in nature. The objects of our thoughts are largely extramental and physical in nature. Some of these objects are intramental and psychic, it is true, but even in this case our thoughts of these intramental realities are not identical with the latter. Is the mental representation a true representation? Can we have assurance that our thoughts are valid representations of their objects, especially if these latter are extramental? Is there an extramental realm at all? May not what we call the world be but a panorama of mental experiences which are purely mind-dependent? Do our perceptions represent mind-independent reality, or do they represent merely intrasubjective phenomena? What is truth and what is its criterion? All these, and many more questions must be answered before we have answered finally the question of the truth of knowledge.

The first of the questions to be answered is: is the universe a mind-independent reality, or is it a mind-dependent reality? The unreflecting man is convinced that through his senses he becomes aware of the existence and nature of an extramental, mind-independent world. That is, he believes that the material universe exists independently of his perception of it, and that he can and does know something about its nature. It is for us to subject these spontaneous certitudes to a critical examination—to see whether or not they are founded on fact. The question to be considered is: Can we have a philosophic certitude for the belief that the data of sense perception reveal the existence and something of the nature of the extramental world? Can we know that an extramental world exists, and can we know what it is? As we might expect, the history of philosophy offers us a plethora of solutions for this mooted question. We may divide them into (1) Realism, (2) Idealism.

REALISM

Realism is a word of multiple meaning. Naturally we prescind here from its signification in literature, art, and the like. Epistemological realism is the theory which maintains that we may have philosophic certitude that an extramental world exists independently of our perception of it, and that some of our judgments concerning the nature and qualities of this world are true. It gives an affirmative answer to the questions proposed above. "Epistemological realism is the view that . . . real objects are sometimes perceived and sometimes not perceived."[1]

This definition stresses the fact that realism insists that reality can exist at moments other than the moment of perception, or of any other conscious experience, and independently of such experience. There are many forms of realism ranging from extreme naïve realism on the one hand

---

[1] This is the definition of realism submitted by the committee on definitions of the American Philosophical Association at the 1911 meeting. *Journal of Phil. Psych. and Scientific Methods*, Vol. VIII, 1911, p. 703.

to hypercritical realism on the other. Naïve realism is the realism professed by those who have given little or no thought to the problem. The naïve realist overlooks the rôle played by the sentient subject in the percipient process, and, as a consequence, often attributes to external realities qualities they do not possess.[2]

Hypercritical realism attributes so much to the percipient subject that it is hardly distinguishable from idealism. Between the two extremes of naïve and hypercritical realism there is critical realism which we shall expound and defend.[3]

Scholastics, old and new, are realists. But although they are in accord on the question of the existence of an extramental world, they, like other realists, differ on the question of how we become aware of this world. The two views on point are (1) perceptionism, and (2) representationism.

Perceptionism. This theory, also called the theory of immediate or presentative sense perception, holds that external reality is apprehended immediately through the senses. There is a medium intervening between the object sensed and the percipient subject, namely the modification of the mind caused by the external object; but this modification (or medium) does not rise to the level of consciousness during perception. It is a medium by which we know reality—it is not a medium which we know. It is a vehicle of knowledge, not an object of knowledge. The mind tends to reality directly and immediately, and it is only by reflection that it becomes aware of the mental state as such. The medium is

---

[2] For a description of naïve realism consult Vance, *op. cit.*, chap. 1; Sellars, *Essentials of Philosophy,* chaps. 2 and 3.

[3] Among the contemporary exponents of realism may be mentioned: Russell, Moore, Alexander, Nunn, Wolf, Hobhouse, Laird, Joad, Reid, Broad, and Hicks, in England; Woodbridge, McGilvery, Fullerton, Rogers, Lovejoy, Pratt, Santayana, Strong, Sellars, Drake, and Whitehead, in this country; Kuelpe, Hartmann, Husserl, and Meinong, in Germany; Lossky, in Russia. A form of realism called neo-realism is fostered by the six American neo-realists, Perry, Montague, Holt, Marvin, Pitkin, and Spaulding. See below p. 156.

not an intermediate representation from which the mind infers the existence of the object; it is nothing but a psychic affection or modification by which the mind is conformed to the object. That there must be such a medium is proved from the fact that we must allow that the external world acts in some way or other on our faculties, and that our perceptions are due to this action or influence. If we do not admit the existence of such a medium then we must admit that our knowledge of the external is either innate or ready-made.[4]

Perceptionism was the theory held by the medieval scholastics and it is held to-day by some of the neo-scholastics.[5]

Representationism. Representationism, or the theory of mediate or inferential sense perception, maintains that the non-Ego is not apprehended immediately. It holds that only the Ego and its states are apprehended immediately, and that because of the "externality" which characterizes some of these states the mind discriminates between the latter and those states which are not "external" and infers that those which are external must have an external cause. In this view that data or objects immediately attained through perception are not extramental, but are intramental objects of the subject's consciousness. Hence representationists essay to justify philosophically the process whereby we transcend these intramental data and achieve a knowledge of extramental reality. They appeal to the principle of causality. The externality of these data must be caused by objects external to the mind, by the non-Ego; there is no other adequate cause for it. Hence the non-Ego exists. We may contrast the perceptionist and

---

[4] St. Thomas, *Summa*, I, q. 85, art. 2.
[5] It is ably propounded by Coffey, *Epistemology*, Vol. II; it finds other supporters in T. Pesch, Farges, Lercher, Boetzkes, Geny, Gredt, Michelitch, Fechner, Schellwein, Klein, Noel, et al. See Gruender, *De Cognitione Sensuum Externorum*, p. 59.

representationist views thus: the former holds that the mind (A) knows the reality (C) immediately (in the sense explained above); the latter holds that the mind (A) knows the mental state (B) immediately but not the reality (C). It can know C only by inferring its existence from B. This is the view to which many neo-scholastics adhere owing to the difficulties which modern science, especially physics and physiology, have raised against the perceptionist theory.[6] We shall give both the perceptionist and representationist proof for the existence of an extramental world.

An Extramental World Exists. Formerly realistic philosophers were wont to spend much effort in proving the existence of a mind-independent world. Up to comparatively recent times the controversy between subjective idealism and realism was sharply debated. But subjective idealism was driven from the field and the contemporary foe of realism is objective idealism, which, despite its name, is a form of epistemological realism.[7]

As Ward writes, "The duality of experience as involving both a subject and an object, an *experiens* and an *expertum*, is no longer questioned by any competent thinker." [8]

Practically all epistemologists are ready to grant that perception is in some sense the revelation of a reality which is external to the percipient subject. However because of the intimate connection between subjective and objective idealism it will not be otiose to set forth the realistic proof for the existence of an extramental world.

Perceptionist proof. All men admit that some of our con-

[6] Among the neo-scholastic supporters of this theory are Vance, Jeannière, Froebes, Gruender, Balzer, Lahr, De Vorges, Stoeckel, and the Louvain school generally. See Gruender, *op. cit.*, p. 12. Mercier's own view seems to be that we cannot affirm with certitude the existence of extramental reality without recourse to the principle of causality. (*Crit. Gener.*, par. 140.)

[7] For idealism, see below, p. 110.

[8] *Hibbert Journal*, Oct., 1924, p. 176.

scious data appear to be external, i.e., they appear to be external to, and other than, the subject of these data. The percepts I have of other men, of trees, of buildings, etc., are characterized by an externality which marks them off as realities existing independently of me and of my perception of them. They seem to be percepts of realities which are not part of my Ego and which do not depend for their existence on my Ego, or on their being thought of. But if they are not external, as they seem to be, why and how do they appear so? The anti-realist must answer this question before he rejects realism. And even if the "why" be answered the "how" cannot be explained. For if there were no external realm of reality how can things be externalized? If external data are not external thy are internal. But if they are internal it is difficult to understand how they are, or can be, externalized. Neither can we understand how we could even grasp the concept of externality, since there is no basis for such a concept on the anti-realist theory. There is no reason for assuming, as some do, that an unconscious part of the Ego externates certain phases of itself.[9]

This is at best an unproved and an unproveable assumption. But granted that there is an unconscious part of the Ego, and that it functions in this way, the question still remains: How can the unconscious Ego which is purely subjective cause an apparent extrasubjectivity of sense data?[10]

Furthermore if there were no external reality the externalization or objectivation of sensations would be inexplicable. It is no explanation to say that we have formed a habit of so doing since the habit presupposes a first externalization and

---

[9] Huxley, *Hume, with Helps to the Study of Berkeley*, p. 96.
[10] "The theory that I make my world by projecting or ejecting my sensations out of my head is an epistemological myth. As James Ward says, if this theory were true then everything would go into my head including the head itself." Leighton, *Man and the Cosmos*, p. 85.

this is quite impossible. Again, an association of internal data cannot result in external data; it can produce but a complexus of internal data.

The findings of introspection confirm the view that the Ego is not an adequate cause for the apparent externality of the data in question. In experiencing our percepts we feel ourselves passive; we feel that they are not of our making. They are our percepts, it is true, and we play a not unimportant part in their production by placing ourselves in suitable circumstances for their occurrence, but we know that their content is not wholly determined by ourselves. The images of my imagination (which are subjective) depend largely on my will, but my perceptions are largely independent of me. I can imagine the Alps but I cannot perceive them here and now. I must put myself in suitable circumstances if I am to perceive them, and in that event, if I open my eyes their perception is forced upon me. The fact that we play a passive rôle in perception and an active rôle in imagining is a commonplace, and it confirms the realistic thesis that the things we perceive are external to us, and being external to us we cannot perceive them unless they are in the field of perception.

But if realities exist which are external to the self there is every reason why they should appear so. They appear external because they are external. And as we shall see when we study idealism there is no reason why they should not be external.

Representationist proof. As we have seen this school employs the principle of causality to prove the existence of an extramental domain of reality. They believe that this principle, "an existing contingent thing (i.e., a being which does not exist by virtue of its essence, which does not contain in its essence the sufficient reason of its existence) necessarily demands a cause," is objectively valid. The necessity and therefore the truth of this judgment is seen from an analysis of its terms.[11]

We are conscious of a changing series of data, some of which appear to be external. Our perceptions of these data are contingent events. They exist therefore by virtue of a cause; they must be caused since they are contingent. But this cause cannot be the self. Therefore there exist, really distinct from the self, realities which in conjunction with the percipient self give rise to our perceptions. The externality and contingency of our data cannot be denied. They come and go, they begin to be and cease to be, they are constantly changing. For example, I am not reading the words now which I was reading a moment ago. Because of their contingency they demand a cause; they are not self-explanatory. But this cause cannot be the Ego. (1) My will has not the power of determining what perceptions I have. I can will to have a perception with all the strength of my volition, yet my willing is powerless to produce it. (2) Neither is my imagination potent enough to produce it. Reflection tells me that there is a great difference between the images brought into consciousness by the imagination and the data of sense perception. The images of the imagination are largely under the control of the will. We can control the order in which they present themselves and we can construct new images as we wish. But percepts are beyond the control of the will. I can, for instance, imagine the color of this paper to be red but I cannot change the

---

[11] Some have objected that the representationist in using this principle at this stage of his proof presupposes the existence of the world, since it is only through our experience of external realities that we come to acquire the concept of contingency. It would seem, however, that a justification of this principle is found in the indisputable flux of our mental states. This flux is an example of contingency, and it is this fact which gives the representationists warrant for the formation of this principle. A knowledge of the external world is not necessary for the formation of the principle of causality.

percept of whiteness that I have. Again, images are faint or weak states, while the data of percepts are strong and vivid states. Reflection tells me that the latter possess a higher degree of definiteness, clearness, and solidity than the former. An imagined dinner is far less satisfactory than one actually eaten. Furthermore, we are conscious that we produce our own images, while in the case of percepts we are conscious of being subjected to impressions made upon us by the non-Ego. Hence the imagination cannot account for the externality which marks our sense data. Since nothing in the Ego can account for the character of these data, since they cannot be accounted for by causes which are subjective or mental, it follows that their cause cannot be ourselves; their cause must be the non-self, therefore the non-self exists.

These are in brief the proofs of the existence of a real, extramental universe offered by the perceptionists and representationists respectively. We may add to these proofs, as confirmatory of the realistic position, the fact that idealism is unable to displace realism. It cannot be shown that realism is false, which means that there is no reason for doubting its truth. It seems true, it squares with the facts revealed by introspection, it cannot be proved to be false. Therefore it is true. Before we begin a discussion of idealism it will be relevant at this juncture to examine the merits of representationism.

CRITICISM: (1) The chief defect of this species of realism is that it contravenes the obvious fact that we perceive external reality directly. We perceive external reality by means of sensations, but the sensations are not perceived. Sensations are not objects of knowledge—they are means of knowledge. When I perceive this book, for example, is it not clear that I perceive the book itself and not my sensations of it? In order to perceive it I must have had some sensations—my eyes saw patches of color, and my hands felt a resistance—

but I did not perceive these sensations directly. I only became aware of them afterwards, i.e., when by reflection I directed my attention to them. Sensations are never perceived directly, and it requires a reflex act of the mind to detect them at all.

The very fact that we distinguish between our sensations of things and the things themselves proves that we are conscious of things rather than our sensations of things, because we can only make a distinction between objects which are in our consciousness. We could not speak of both sensation and object unless we were conscious of both sensation and object. Hence one cannot be the other, and it is a contradiction in terms to say that we do not know an object but only its mental representation. The representationist confounds the object of perception with the means of perception.

The view that we perceive our sensations is the heritage of a philosophical prejudice which goes back to Descartes and Locke. It seems incredible that man's daily experience should not have dispossessed this theory which holds that all we can know is our subjective states—but it still persists. Representationism is an attempt to retain the initial assumption of this prejudice and still avoid its logical conclusion—idealism.[12]

(2) If a *tertium quid* intervenes between the mind and the object, and if from a knowledge of this the mind infers the existence and nature of the reality, how can we ever know that our knowledge is valid? As Berkeley argues against Locke, "How can we possibly know whether our ideas agree with what *ex hypothesi* cannot be known at all?" Knowledge which is true must correspond with its object. But on this theory we cannot know the object and hence we cannot know if there is a correspondence or not. Once we limit the mind's

---

[12] On this point consult, Walker, *op. cit.*, chap. 1; Lossky, *The Intuitive Basis of Realism*, Eng. trans., p. 37; Spencer, *Principles of Psychology*, p. 373; Fullerton, *The World We Live In*, p. 113; Drake et al., *Essays in Critical Realism*, p. 90; Laird, *A Study in Realism*, p. 15.

power to know directly to the Ego and its states we cannot get beyond the limits we have set. Furthermore, if the materials of knowledge are but mental states of the knowing subject, it follows that even the thought of the existence of an external world could never have occurred to the mind. It is of no avail to invoke the principle of causality since it does not tell us where we can find the cause of our data, nor does it tell us our search must be successful. If all I can know is the subjective then I should naturally be compelled to find the cause of these data in the subjective order. Again, I cannot know that there is an extrasubjective order that can function causally, since I have not proved—and cannot prove on this theory—that the principle of causality holds good in the objective order. The fact that the principle of causality holds good in the subjective order is no proof that it holds good in the objective order, and it cannot be proved to hold good in the objective order unless the existence of the world is granted—which is the point to be proved. From the very nature of the case, therefore this theory cannot establish its position.

(3) Another objection to representationism is that based on the numerical duality between the space occupied by the inferred (or real) object and the space occupied by the perceived object. If the mind can only experience its own mental states then it must infer the existence and qualities of the real object from these states. The object inferred is never the object perceived. The former is the cause of the latter—it is not the latter. If this is so, the inferred object does not occupy the same space as the perceived object because numerical duality implies occupancy of different spaces. But the question arises: Where is the "real" space occupied by the "real" object? The object cannot be in perceived space because that is subjective while it is objective. And yet I cannot get beyond perceived space because on this theory

all I perceive is subjective. I cannot even think of a space that is discontinuous with perceived space. If the inferred object does not exist in perceived space, where does it exist? Idealists say it does not exist at all—and they draw their conclusions from premises admitted by representationism.[13]

Perceptionism has its difficulties as well as representationism. The consideration of these difficulties will be postponed until after an examination of idealism.

[13] Consult Coffey, *Epist.*, Vol. II, pp. 26-36, 58-63; Joad, *Essays in Common Sense Philosophy*, chap. 1; Sellars, *op. cit.*, p. 52.

CHAPTER X

SUBJECTIVE IDEALISM

In the preceding chapter we attempted to offer a rational justification for man's spontaneous convictions as regards the existence of an extramental world. We now propose an examination of the anti-realistic view. Do the idealists prove their contention? Are the arguments they adduce sufficient to overthrow the realistic theory? Because of these arguments should we abandon realism? If we can prove these arguments are fallacious we have buttressed the position we have established above. Our belief is that the arguments of idealism do not disprove realism.

DEFINITION OF IDEALISM

Idealism like realism is a term of wide connotation. We disregard here the meanings it has in other fields of knowledge and confine ourselves to epistemological idealism.[1] In this usage idealism is opposed to epistemological realism. The realist holds that in sense perception we can have reasoned certitude of the existence of a reality distinct from the modifications of the perceiving mind and existing independently of the perception of it. Idealism doubts or denies that anything beyond the Ego and its states can be an object

---

[1] For the various meanings of idealism consult the *Catholic Encyclopedia*, Vol. VII, p. 634; Baldwin, *Dictionary of Philosophy and Psychology*, Vol. I, p. 500. Epistemological idealism has nothing to do with ideals. It has to do with ideas—and hence it should be more properly called ideaism—or mentalism, as some prefer. See Hoernlé, *Idealism as a Philosophy*, p. 45.

ELEMENTS OF EPISTEMOLOGY

of knowledge; it doubts or denies that external reality can be known to exist.[2]

It is the system which holds to the "negation of anything except ideas; or to put the same thing in an affirmative way, the affirmation of the unknowableness of anything except ideas."[3]

It maintains that "the real object cannot exist at other moments independently of any perception."[4]

Idealism is sometimes called subjectivism because it affirms that only the psychic states of the knowing subject can be the objects of knowledge.

KINDS OF IDEALISM

Absolute, or psychological, idealism denies the existence of any reality distinct from the mental representation of the knowing subject. It holds that the sole object of knowledge is the conscious states of the subject. Closely akin to this view is solipsism—the theory that the conscious self is the only reality; the possibility of the existence of other similar but really distinct conscious selves cannot be justified intellectually. Relative idealism admits that we can have philosophical certitude for the existence of some reality distinct from the Ego. It restricts unduly, however, the scope of this certitude as well as the objects of this certitude. Berkeley's immaterialism is relatively idealistic. Spencer's transfigured realism is also a type of this kind of idealism. Positivism and phenomenalism, sometimes called empirical or phenomenal idealism, deny the existence of any intra- or extrasubjective substance, and hence they are species of relative idealism.

---

[2] If idealism doubts the possibility of a knowledge of the non-Ego it is called skeptical idealism; if it denies this possibility it is called dogmatic.

[3] Mercier, *Origins*, Eng. trans., p. 41.

[4] This is the definition proposed by the committee on definitions of the Am. Phil. Assoc., in 1911. See the *Journal of Phil., etc.*, Vol. VIII, 1911, p. 703.

Objective idealism must also be noted since in one form or another it is one of the most widespread philosophies of our day. It differs from subjective idealism in that it denies that the external world is but the ideas of a finite conscious being. It grants that the world is objective as regards the individual but maintains that it and all other entities are in some way psychical or mental in nature, being identified with the mind of an Absolute, Self, or Spirit. Subjective idealism makes the world subjective in its being, while this theory admits the objectivity of the world with reference to finite conscious beings such as ourselves. It says in effect, the world is idea but it is not my idea. The world exists, but its ultimate nature is mental since it is a part of the great all-inclusive Absolute. Epistemologically it is a species of realism.

History of Idealism

The history of idealism begins with Descartes and Locke—both of whom were realists. The main current of English and continental idealism has the latter as its source.[5]

It followed his assumption that the mind is primarily limited in knowledge to a perception of its own subjective states, or, as he puts it, that "the mind in all its thoughts and reasonings hath no other immediate object but its own ideas which it alone does or can contemplate."[6]

This is the presupposition of many modern philosophers; they have accepted this statement as embodying the essential nature of knowledge.[7]

---

[5] For the history of idealism see Mercier, *Origins,* chaps. 1 and 2.
[6] *Essay,* 4, 1, 1.
[7] The number of idealistic philosophers is legion. Confining our attention to the more modern we may mention the names of the following: in England, Green, the Cairds, Bradley, Mackintosh, Pringle-Pattison, Lord Haldane, McTaggart, Bosanquet, Hibben, Adamson, Hodgson; in Germany, Lotze, Bache, Paulsen, Busse, Liebmann, Cassirer, Eucken, Cohen, Natorp, Krause, Windelband, Schuppe, Rickert, Mach, Verworen, Dilthy; in France, Renouvier, Lachelier, Sabatier, Weber, Brunschvicg,

ELEMENTS OF EPISTEMOLOGY 113

Idealism is a system born of reflection. Men spontaneously are realists. They are impelled into idealism by the difficulties of realism, which difficulties they believe cannot be answered by the realistic theory. It is for us to consider the main arguments set forth by the idealists which they hold show at once the impossibility of the realistic theory and the truth of their own.

The Main Argument for Idealism. This is the stock argument of idealists. It is based on the cardinal principle of that system—the principle of immanence. The principle is this: the object of knowledge is necessarily in the knowing subject, and the latter does not, and cannot become aware of any reality transcending himself. The data of my consciousness cannot be really external to, or other than, my consciousness. Even if the existence of extrasubjective reality be granted, it is impossible for us to become conscious of it, since we can only become conscious of reality in so far as it is present in our consciousness. Hence when the realist says that he perceives objects which are external to, and independent of, his consciousness he is uttering a self-contradiction. The realist may doubt or deny that the existence of an object consists of its being perceived but he cannot doubt or deny that the only things of whose existence our perceptions assure us are sense data, and that these are known and hence are "in" the mind, since nothing can be known unless it is in some mind. We certainly cannot perceive a being which is not in our mind, which is distinct from, and unrelated to, our mind. Should such a being exist it would be unperceived and unperceivable. To clarify this by an example: I perceive a tree.

Bazaillas, LeRoy, Boutroux, Fouillée; in Italy, Caritoni, Croce, Gentile; in this country, Emerson, Harris, Everett, Royce, Albee, Ladd, J. Watson, Ormond, Bowne, Creighton, Calkins, Wenley, Gardiner, Tufts, Bakewell, Hocking; in South Africa, Hoernlé. This list is far from complete. Many of the above profess widely divergent systems, but they all have idealistic tendencies at least.

The perception of the tree is in my consciousness. I could not perceive the tree unless it were in my consciousness since it is obvious that I can perceive only what I perceive. I cannot perceive the unperceived, and I cannot therefore perceive a tree which is not in my consciousness, of which I am not aware, which is independent of, and external to my consciousness.[8]

CRITICISM: We do not maintain that the data of our consciousness are unrelated to, or independent of, or external to, our consciousness. We are at one with the idealists in holding that such a theory is self-contradictory. We cannot perceive an unperceivable world. The data of our consciousness must be data *of* our consciousness. It is absurd and contradictory to suppose that we can know unknowable things, see unseeable things, and hear unhearable things. But it is not absurd or contradictory to hold, as we do, that a reality can exist unperceived by any human mind and that the same reality can be afterwards perceived.[9]

In other words, it is not absurd to suppose that a thing can belong both to the order of ideas and to the real order, i.e., that the same reality can exist and can be known to exist. It is not self-contradictory to hold that a thing can be and can be known. The truth that an extramental reality to be known must be cognitively one with the knowing subject makes the knowledge of the object and not the reality of the object dependent on the knower. Idealists have confused the knowledge of reality with reality. Reverting to the example used above, all that an idealist can logically prove is that the thought of the tree must be in the mind (if it is to be

[8] See Bain, *Mental Science*, p. 197, for a clear statement of the idealist argument. Cf., also Bradley, *Appearance and Reality*, pp. 144-145, "We perceive, on reflection, that to be real, or even barely to exist, must be to fall within Sentience. Sentient experience, in short, is reality, and what is not this is not real. . . . Anything in no sense felt or perceived becomes to me quite unmeaning."

[9] See Maher, *op. cit.*, p. 111.

known)—not the tree itself. If put into syllogistic form the fallacy committed by idealists is clearly seen.

What is subjective (dependent on the mind for existence) is not an extramental reality but an idea.
All objects of which we are aware are subjective (present to our consciousness).
Therefore all objects of which we are aware are not extramental objects but ideas.

This is an instance of the fallacy of four terms. Or more simply, idealism rests on a fallacious conversion. From the truth that "All objects which depend on consciousness for their existence are objects for the knowing subject," it is inferred by a simple conversion that "All things that are objects for a knowing subject are dependent on consciousness for their existence." It is a law of logic that a universal affirmative proposition must be converted accidentally. The correct converse is, "Some things that are objects for a knowing subject are dependent for their existence."[10] Idealism proves something all admit, viz., that we can never be conscious of an object of which we are not conscious; it can prove nothing regarding the existence or non-existence of objects not in our consciousness.[11]

The Second Argument for Idealism. Besides misconceiving the realistic position the idealists are guilty of a gratuitous assumption, an assumption on which their whole theory of knowledge rests, viz., that the mind cannot know extramental reality. We admit that whatever is known must be

---

[10] MacIntosh, *The Problem of Knowledge*, p. 96.
[11] MacGregor, *Hibbert Journal*, 1906, p. 788, puts the failure of the idealistic argument thus: Idealism has proved that "reality" cannot be thought as existing, independently of thought; but it has not proved that "reality" cannot be thought, as existing independently of thought. On this point see Russell, *op. cit.*, chap. 4; Perry, *Present Philosophical Tendencies*, p. 113; Spaulding, *op. cit.*, p. 233; Coffey, *Epist.*, Vol. II, p. 46; Joad, *Modern Philosophy*, p. 9.

related to, and in cognitive union with, the knowing mind. This simply means, as we have seen, that the perception or apprehension of the object is dependent on mind; it means no mind—no perception or knowledge. It does not mean that the reality is dependent on, or immanent in, the knower. Idealists refuse to admit that our minds can become aware of realities other than themselves and their states. They ask, "How can a mind transcend itself and know an extramental reality?" and on our inability to answer they claim that the mind cannot know the extramental. But we claim that the statement, "The mind cannot know the extramental," is neither an a priori nor a self-evident truth; it cannot be proved empirically. They find no difficulty in admitting that a percipient subject can know intramental reality, and yet they cannot explain how a subject can know his own conscious states any more than we can explain how he knows the extramental. The "how" of our knowledge of the intramental is just as difficult to explain as is the "how" of our knowledge of the extramental. If it is legitimate for them to ask, "How can the extrasubjective be known?" it is just as legitimate for us to ask, "How can the intrasubjective be known?"

It is wholly arbitrary to limit the question to the one kind of reality. If a question is to be put at all, it should take the form, "How is it possible to know anything?" But this question has only to be put to be discarded. For it amounts to a demand to *explain* knowledge; and any answer to it would involve the derivation of knowledge from what was not knowledge. . . .[12]

The limitations of our present discussion should be kept clearly in mind. We have endeavored to show that the arguments which idealists put forth in support of their theory are invalid; they do not prove their point. The burden of proof

[12] Prichard, *op. cit.*, p. 124; see also Maher, *op. cit.*, p. 115; Drake et al., *op. cit.*, p. 99.

rests on idealism. We are realists by nature and we should not relinquish realism until it is proved to be untenable. We have not attempted to disprove idealism directly. But we maintain that there is no reason why a system which is based on invalid arguments, and which is highly artificial and difficult of adoption on practice, should be held, especially in view of the fact that none of its arguments refute the realistic theory, which latter works in practice, and hence should not be rejected except for good reason.

Difficulties of Idealism

Idealism and solipsism. Solipsism is the view that nothing but the self exists; no other men exist except the thinker. It would seem that this is the logical outcome of subjective idealism. For if it is true that there is no extramental reality, then the bodies of other men as distinct from the subject do not exist. Yet it is only because other men have bodies that we come to know them; it is through their speech, writing, gestures, etc.—all of which imply a material organism—that they can be present to our consciousness. Mind cannot communicate directly with mind. "I cannot transcend my experience; and experience must be *my* experience. From this it follows that nothing beyond myself exists, for what is experience is its (the self's) states." [13]

Some idealists have the courage to admit this but most of them temper their idealism at the expense of their logic.

Idealism and science. There seems to be an absolute incompatibility between idealism and science, so much so that the logical subjective idealist cannot assent to the teachings of modern science. The physical sciences are based on the assumption that matter exists, that tri-dimensional bodies exist and act independently of human observation. The qualities and activities scientists attribute to these bodies show

[13] Bradley, *op. cit.*, p. 248.

that the latter are not sensations or possibilities of sensations. Purely mental existents do not attract each other with a force that varies inversely with the square of the distance between them; neither do they develop from forests into coal-beds.[14]

Some scientists have essayed to retain their science while professing idealism, Mach and Pearson for example, but they are inconsistent in so doing.[15]

Idealism and psychology. Psychologists, both realistic and idealistic, admit a correlation between mental processes and brain processes. They assume the existence of the body with its brain and nervous system as extramental realities; they then prove that it is through the functioning of the nervous system and sense organs that they sense reality. But when the idealistic psychologist turns to epistemology he endeavors to show how muscular feelings and the like give rise to a belief in extramental reality. He goes on to prove that this feeling is illusory, that there are no extramental realities, that everything is intramental and subjective. It follows that the human body with its sense organs and nervous system is subjective. This entails the absurdity that a mental state is the subjective aspect of a nerve process which itself is but a group of sensations—and in no way material. Thought is a function of the brain, and the brain, like the rest of the physical universe, is but a plexus of mental states. These two tenets are mutually destructive. Hence the incompatibility between idealism and psychology.

[14] Maher, *op. cit.*, p. 113; Mivart, *On Truth*, p. 79; *Groundwork of Science*, p. 49.
[15] Broad, *Perception, Physics and Reality*, chap. 3.

CHAPTER XI

OBJECTIVE IDEALISM

Because of the complexity of this species of idealism and because of the novelty of its epistemology, it can best be grasped if portrayed against the background of its origins. Its roots lie in Kant's phenomenalism. He taught that the noumenon is unknowable; that the phenomenon is all the mind can attain. He also held the doctrine of transcendental apperception. Human minds function in the same way. Everywhere and always they arrive at the same true conclusions. The sense material out of which they build their knowledge varies for different minds but this material is combined and arranged in the same way and with the same results. In this way he explained that the laws of mathematics, for example, are the same for all men. He accounted for the universality of knowledge by the harmonic synthesizing of individual minds, which he styled transcendental apperception.

His successors centered their attention on these two doctrines—the doctrine of the noumena and transcendental apperception. If space and time and subjective, if reason determines the phenomenon, if it constitutes nature, what becomes of that which is given to the mind? Kant held that the latter was a presentment of the thing-in-itself, but he insisted that the thing-in-itself could not fall within the range of reason. But how, then, later thinkers asked, can the thing-in-itself be known to be an agent? How can we conceive it to be a substance? It is more logical to put the noumenon into the mind with the phenomenon, to make it the product of our faculties of representation like the phenomenon. Thus for them the matter as well as the form of cognition is derived from the structure of the self. In this view the self not only aids in the production of phenomena, as Kant said, but it creates them.

Kant had given but little thought to his doctrine of transcendental apperception, but this superindividual consciousness, which is the same for all men, occupies a preponderating place in the thought of his successors. The Kantian position had evident flaws. The human kind, he declared, was the law-giver to nature. Before reality can be known it must pass through the mind with its mechanism of categories and the like, and to that extent it must be regarded as something built up and unified by the mind. Man does not create the world, it is true, but before he can know it, he must recreate it out of the sensations it impresses upon him. To the obvious criticism that man is subject to the laws which govern the world of reality, and that these laws are seemingly not of his making, the Kantian reply was a distinction between the "transcendental self" and the "empirical self." It is not the latter, the finite mind of the individual, which is the legislator for nature, but the former which is not an object of the empirical world at all, since it is not subject to the intuitions of time and space, nor to the dominion of the categories. Of its intrinsic nature we can know nothing since it belongs to the noumenal order. All we can know of it is its representations in this world of phenomena—one of which is its phenomenal duplicate—the empirical self. The latter, since it is but a phenomenon, is subject to the same laws as any other object of the phenomenal order.[1]

---

[1] This conception of the "transcendental self" has, of course, no basis in experience. It is an invention necessitated by the dialectic of Kant's system.

Kant himself did not deny that transcendental selves were independent of each other but his followers interpreted his transcendental apperception and his "transcendental self" theory in a monistic sense, arguing that the transcendental self was the same for all men. These selves are not, for them, independent and individual. They constitute one universal and absolute self. We know that the different truths which our minds hold concerning the universe are independent of our private opinions. They impress themselves on us as truths which we do not make but which we find already established. There must therefore be a universal mind whose truths about nature are definite and final. In this way the transcendental self was substantialized and became the subject of a universal consciousness, the Absolute. This absolute self, or Absolute as it is usually called, furnishes not only the form but the matter of our experience. It constitutes reality—it is reality. Thought and reality are one. The categories do not constitute the phenomenal world but the real world. Thus the principle which for Kant prevailed in the field of the mental became a principle in the field of reality; thought and reality were identified. The thought that constitutes reality, it must be understood, is not the thought of the individual but the thought of the universal thinker. Since thought is immanent in a mind, the universe, which is thought, is immanent in the mind of the Absolute. In this way the universe is rescued from the instability of the human mind; it thus acquires permanency and order from the Absolute. The gap between thought and reality is closed—they are one, and the thing-in-itself, the bug-bear of philosophers, disappears.[2]

[2] It is difficult to crystallize the tenets of objective idealism. Not all of this school are monists, although the logic of Kantianism leans that way. Some of them profess pluralism, e.g., James Ward, Howison, and McTaggart. But whether monistic or pluralistic it is of the essence of objective idealism to hold that the universe is made up of mind, or minds, and the experience of mind. For individual statements of this species of idealism consult: Hegel, *Philosophy of Mind,* trans. by W.

CRITICISM: Objective idealism in one form or another has been for some time the "genteel tradition" in Continental, English, and American philosophy. The dominance it has so long enjoyed has waned somewhat under the vigorous attacks of a resurgent realism, but it still holds a position of prestige in contemporary thought. Its many-sidedness, impinging as it does on the fields of practically all the philosophic disciplines, has made it the target for much criticism. We shall confine ourselves to an examination of its epistemology.

First criticism. The gist of one of the main arguments of idealists is that the unity of knowledge cannot be explained except on the hypothesis of a universal consciousness. Our knowledge is characterized by unity; there must, therefore, be a universal consciousness which makes our knowledge possible.[3]

The initial criticism of this protean philosophy is based on its use—or misuse—of the phrase "unity of consciousness." This much-used phrase is capable of two widely divergent interpretations.

First, introspection shows me that I am an individual being, the seat of various mental phenomena, and that these latter are held together in some way—by some sort of a bond which links together, however vaguely, the states of which I am conscious, into a unity. In this sense there is in me a real unity of consciousness. The second meaning attached to this phrase is very different from the above. When I know things they are in cognitional contact with me, they enter intentionally into my mind, they have an ideal existence in my mind.

Wallace; Green, *Prolegomena to Ethics;* Royce, *The Spirit of Modern Philosophy;* Bosanquet, *The Principle of Individuality and Value;* Calkins, *The Persistent Problems of Philosophy;* Adams, *Idealism and the Modern Age;* Howison, *The Limits of Evolution;* Bradley, *Appearance and Reality;* McTaggart, *Studies in Hegelian Cosmology;* Hoernlé, *Idealism as a Philosophy.*

[3] See, for example, Green, *Prolegomena to Ethics,* pars. 59-65.

They are objects of my consciousness, which is one, as I am one. Since all reality that is knowable is, or can be, that of which I am conscious, since it enters into my unity of consciousness, it may also be called a unity of consciousness. In this usage the connotation of the phrase is transferred from the consciousness which knows to that which the consciousness knows. For purposes of clarity, and in conformity with ordinary usage, this second meaning should be expressed as the "unity of knowledge," and not as the "unity of consciousness."

It is the second meaning which bulks large in idealistic thought, and the general fallacy which underlies the idealist position will be clearly seen if we denominate the objects of our knowledge as the "unity of knowledge" and not as the "unity of consciousness." The unity of our knowledge which is an admitted fact, is no warrant for the assertion that there is a general, or universal, unity of consciousness. All that can be concluded from the fact that we all are unities of consciousness is that reality is intelligible, not that it is intelligent—or that it is a unity of consciousness in itself. Reality is intelligible, i.e., reality is known to us as a unified whole. The unity of the cosmos is objective; it presents itself to me, and I cognize it as such. But my knowledge of the universe is not the universe. My knowledge of the universe is a logical construction based on my experience of the universe, and it by no means follows that because my knowledge is in the logical order that the universe is likewise a logical and not an ontological entity. All that right reason can conclude from the fact that our knowledge reveals the universe as a unity is that the universe is a unity, and that it is capable of being known as such. If the conclusion is drawn that the unity of the known universe proves that the universe is an existent unitary mind, or Absolute, or that thought and reality are identical, it far outruns its premises.

Second criticism. The basic tenet of objective idealism is the dependence of being on a mind, or Absolute, which envelops both the physical and psychic orders. Consciousness is an essential and necessary condition for being. We have discussed the value of this idealist assumption above.[4]

It is true that things to be known have to come within the field of the mental—they must enter the circle of the psychic. All known things are known. But it by no means follows that "all things are known." Things may be and be known. A reality may belong to two or more different contexts or systems without prejudice to its identity. The fields of knowledge and reality can overlap, and the field of knowledge in overlapping the field of reality does not interfere with or condition the latter. For example, the letter "e" is the second letter of the word "desk" and the fifth letter of the word "table." Its position in the first word in no way interferes with its position in the second word. It has a multiple particularity, and it would be obviously incorrect to define it by its position in either of these words. Similarly it is equally incorrect to define things as "objects of awareness." They are things whether they are thought of or not, and to define them in such a way is to sin against logic. Idealism must prove that thought is the essence of reality—and this it has not done.

This typically idealist fallacy is seen in the idealist doctrine on the categories. Both realists and idealists hold that we think in categories. The idealist, reverting to his basic assumption, maintains that, since categories cannot be known without being thought of, they cannot exist without being thought, and forthwith makes them a part of the mental mechanism. He avers that the categories condition reality. The realist rejoins that the categories can exist without being thought of, and he allocates them to the world of reality.

[4] See p. 113.

He holds that the mind finds the categories in reality; it does not place them there. In this, apart from all other considerations, his position is just as reasonable as that of the idealist, for if true knowledge must conform to the reality it represents then knowledge must be determined by reality. Hence if there are categories in reality there must be categories in the mind, but only in the mind in so far as the thought of mind is representative of reality, not in the mind as mind. Not only is the realistic view rational, but in view of the fact that the idealist commits a logical fallacy in arguing to the subjectivity of the categories, it is easily preferred.[5]

Third criticism. Objective idealism aimed to rescue idealism in general from the reproach of solipsism. That a thoroughgoing subjectivism logically ends in solipsism is admitted to-day. Defenders of objective idealism maintain that their doctrine of the Absolute has thus rendered irrelevant the usual anti-idealist arguments. The realist answers that the introduction of the Absolute but adds to the difficulties of idealism instead of lessening them. The arguments that establish the essential doctrine of idealism, viz., the relativity of existence to thought, if they prove anything, prove only that an object depends for its existence, not upon experience in general, but upon this or that human experience. If these arguments are valid they make the introduction of a super-finite or absolute experience unnecessary. If they are invalid there is no reason for supposing that things depend for their existence upon any experience. It is illogical to use an argument to prove the identity of thought with reality, and then to repudiate it to prove that an Absolute exists. The very error, in other words, which idealism corrects is indispensable for its own initial assumption. Objective idealism must either reject its subjectivistic premises, in which case it must view reality from a non-idealistic standpoint,

[5] See Perry, *Present Philosophical Tendencies*, p. 158.

or it must accept it, and then it stands condemned by its own arguments.[6]

Again, the existence of the Absolute entails certain epistemological difficulties. The Absolute is either knowable by human minds or it is unknowable by them. If it is knowable it is a part of the experience of human minds. And since it falls within this experience there is no warrant for our concluding that it exists outside the experience of these minds (i.e., on idealistic grounds). The logical implication is that the Absolute is non-existent. If, on the other hand, it is unknowable because it falls outside the sphere of human experience, then we cannot know even that it exists. It is reduced to the status of a merely possible being whose existence cannot be verified.[7]

Fourth criticism. An idealist argument made much of by most modern idealists of the Hegelian school has to do with the nature of relations. It is alleged that there are no such things as external relations, i.e., relations which are extrinsic to the terms they relate. Relations are parts or states of their terms. They penetrate and possess their terms so that the latter cannot be separated from them and retain their existence. Any single object is, if taken by itself, meaningless; it is meaningful only when it is taken in its context. And since a thing which is devoid of its full meaning is not really a thing, we may say that a thing is a reality in the strict sense of that term when it is taken in conjunction with its context. The context must be assumed to be part of a thing, if the thing is to be an entity. For example, this book is smaller than some books and larger than others; its color is the same

[6] That much objective idealism, despite its disavowals, derives its fundamental premises from subjective idealism, is admitted by Pringle-Pattison, a member of the idealistic school. ". . . This transcendental idealism is just Berkeleian idealism *in excelsis,* Berkeleianism universalized and applied on a cosmic scale; and the reasoning is, therefore, of the same circular character." *Idea of God,* p. 193.

[7] See Joad, *Modern Philosophy,* p. 10.

as the color of some books and different from the color of others, etc. Unless it stood in all these relations to other books, and to all other realities, it would not be this particular book. Hence the relations which it has to other things help to constitute the nature of the book. Its relations are not independent of it—they are states of the book and the things to which it is related, and they make the book and these things what they are. Everything in the universe is related to everything else. Hence the nature of each forms part of the nature of all; nature is an interrelated whole—the Absolute.

Not only are relations constitutive of reality but they are the product of mind. If the universe is a vast unified system of relations it must have been made so by a Mind. Relations require a Relater—things cannot relate themselves, neither can they unite themselves. I am aware that the relations which I find in the world are not made by my mind or by minds like mine. They are made, therefore by the Absolute Mind.[8]

The realist contends that relations are external, that they do not constitute reality, that related terms acquire from their relations an additional character, it is true, but that this latter does not condition or alter the essential character they already have. If this were not the case we would not know the essence of a reality unless we were cognizant of all its relations. This seems to be too patent a violation of common sense. Reverting to the example of the book, the reason that it stands in various relations to other books and to other realities is because it is a particular book independently of these relations. If it were not the book it is, it would no thave these relations. If it were its relations, as the idealists say, then we would be committed to the view that the relations we call the book stand in relations to certain other relations. We would

[8] For a typical exposition of this argument see Green, *Prolegomena to Ethics*, pars. 28, 30, 32, 51, 69.

have a universe of relations—with nothing to be related. The conception that relations are something *in vacuo,* and that they relate nothing is quite unthinkable.⁹

Modern realists have symbolized their theory in what is called the axiom of external relations: in the proposition "the term 'a' is in the relation 'R' to the term 'b', aR in no degree constitutes b, nor does Rb constitute a, nor does R constitute either a or b."¹⁰

The Externality of Relations. An analysis of the realistic teaching on the nature of relations will serve to convince us that there is nothing essentially incompatible in the concept of external relations. In the first place, a relation is not a physical nexus which joins two objects together, and thus unifies them. A relation is not an entity capable of existing by itself or in something else. It is rather a reference of one reality to another—this latter being the term of the relation. It is, as Aristotle styled it, a "toward something"—not a thing.¹¹

In every relation there are three elements, the subject of the relation, the term to which the subject is referred, and the ground of the relation. The latter is the cause or reason of the subject's being related to the term. It is patent that some relations belong to the purely logical order, viz., relations between concepts, and between all purely logical entities.

But it is just as evident that there are real relations also, relations which are not constituted by thought, but which are found by the mind already existing, and which are, therefore, not mental products. When the three elements of a relation are real, the relation is real. Anyone who is not imbued with the idealistic prepossession that the mind is constitutive of reality and therefore of relations, cannot deny that two

---
⁹ See Joad, *Mind and Matter,* p. 98.
¹⁰ See Montague, *op. cit.,* p. 345.
¹¹ *I Categ.* 5, 1.

men of the same size are really equal in size, and that two men of different heights are really unequal in size, i.e., that the relations of equality and inequality are objective states of affairs which the mind does not create but which it discovers.[12]

Are Relations the Product of Mind? The view that relations are the product of mind did not originate with the objective idealists; it goes back to the Kantian theory of a spontaneous, non-sensuous, active reason. Meaning in this hypothesis is a synthesis; synthesis is a relating, and relating requires the act of a mind. It is true that meaning implies a connection—and that isolation makes meaning impossible. But does it follow that togetherness is but a fabrication of the mind? May not things be found together by the mind, as well as put together by the mind? "The conception that connection is only the mind's carpentry, or that it cannot be discovered in things, is a mere dogma which should never have lived."[13]

It is not unthinkable that relations exist extramentally; at least no valid reasons can be adduced against their extramental existence.[14]

Idealists apply their doctrine of the internality of relations to the knowledge relation. It is an easy step from this theory to the correlative view that the relation of knowledge which exists between a mind and an object is a relation which affects the character of the object known in an essential way. The knowledge process really constitutes the character and

[12] St. Thomas, *Comment. in Sentent.*, 1, dist. 26, q. 2, art. 1; *De Potentia*, q. 7, art. 11; *Summa*, pars. 1a, q. 13, art. 7; 1, q. 9, art. 27, ad 1am; Coffey, *Ontology*, p. 332.

[13] Laird, *A Study in Realism*, pp. 32-33.

[14] On the question of relations consult, Walker, *op. cit.*, passim; Perry, *op. cit.*, p. 319; Spaulding, "The Logical Structure of Self-Refuting Systems," *Phil. Review*, Vol. XIX, 1910, p. 276; *The New Rationalism*, p. 176; Russell, *Principles of Mathematics*, p. 90; "The Monistic Theory of Truth," in *Philosophical Essays;* "On the Nature of Truth," *Proceedings of the Arist. Soc.*, 1907, N.S., Vol. VII, p. 28.

being of the object to which it is related. But if relations are external, and if, in particular, the knowledge relation is external, then the knowing of an object does not constitute it. After all, knowing is knowing, and not making. This argument in favor of the externality of relations does not prove that the knowledge relation might not be an exception, that it might not be an internal relation. Only an empirical examination will reveal whether it is an internal relation or not. Idealists are wrong in maintaining that the mere fact that knowledge is a relation proves that the known is dependent upon the mind for its existence and nature.

What does reflection tell us of the supposed internality of the cognitive relation? It is true that anything that can be known has the relation of being a possibly known reality to any consciousness that can know it. But any new qualities which this reality gains by reason of its being known in no way negate the properties it had before it was known. It has these latter qualities after it is known just as it had them before it was known. The only change in it is that it is now "known" whereas before it was "unknown." The passing of an object in or out of consciousness does not alter its nature. It is what it is whether it is known or unknown.[15]

Bradley's Criticism of Relations. Before we leave the thorny problem of relations we should note one of Bradley's devastating criticisms of the realistic doctrine of the externality of relations, a criticism which some modern idealists regard as final.[16]

He argues thus: if relations are real we must posit the existence of something which mediates between the relation

---

[15] The failure of the idealistic proof in this regard is admitted by Pringle-Pattison ". . . it seems to confirm our view of the fallacious character of any direct argument from the conditions of knowledge to the theorem of the All-Thinker and of the universe as the system of his thought." *Op. cit.*, p. 199.

[16] *Appearance and Reality*, p. 25.

and each of the related terms, i.e., we must posit the existence of a new entity which relates the relation to each of the related extremes. This new entity must be related to the relation, which relating requires the positing of another new relating entity. On the realistic view, therefore, we are committed to a theory of an infinite number of relations. In other words, if a relation is real, then it is clear that A cannot be related to B by R, since A must be related to R by a new relation, R1; the latter in turn must be related to R by R2, and so on.

Bradley's criticism of the theory of external relations is inept. If a relation relates, and that seems to be the basic and essential characteristic of a relation, it does not need another relation to relate it to its terms. A relation relates— it is not related. Why then posit the intercalation of intermediary relating agencies?

Fifth criticism. This criticism is directed against monistic idealism. Monism in any form has always had to face a number of well known difficulties, both in the arguments it uses to prove its position, and in the position it sustains. Overlooking the logic of its proof let us admit the truth of its conclusion, i.e., that there is an Absolute which is in everything and which is everything. The Absolute is one, real, and true. However the universe we know presents a different picture to us. The universe we know is everything the Absolute is not. It does not appear to be one but many. There is in the universe illusion as well as reality, and error as well as truth. How explain the cleavage between the reality and the appearance? If the universe is really one how does it present itself to us as richly variegated? The answer is sometimes made that the apparent variety and plurality is temporarily externated by the Absolute who will reabsorb them in the future. But in that event the potency to generate multiplicity is in the Absolute. It follows that the Absolute is not a complete, essential unity, but a unity with a power for generating multiplicity. Multiplicity is in the unity, potentially at least. In other words, the Absolute is not really one.

The monist cannot urge that the difference between things is an illusion, that things are really one—their multiplicity being an illusion of our minds, because in that case he must explain our error in thinking them to be many. Our error puts falsity into a true universe, and error is just as difficult to explain as is multiplicity. Monism always breaks down when it endeavors to bridge the gap between reality and appearance, and monistic idealism suffers the fate of monism in general when it attempts to bridge the same gap.[17]

It is evident that the existence of the Absolute is a mere postulate. The idealists, no more than any other school of philosophers, have any experience of the Absolute. The existence of the Absolute must be posited if reality necessarily depends on a mind. It is this reality-experience doctrine which is the essential weakness of this system. As a matter of fact the data of experience contradict this idealistic tenet. Any mind which is not sicklied o'er with the pale cast of idealism experiences the universe as mind-independent and plural.[18]

The universe gives no evidence of being an appearance or adjectival mode of an absolute thinker. That idealists experience it as mind-independent and plural is shown by their efforts to prove that it is mind-dependent and non-plural.

Idealism has ever pleaded for a spiritualistic interpretation of the universe. It has ever decried naturalism, and for this it has merited acclaim. Its merits, however, should not blind

---

[17] Monistic idealism also has difficulty in attempting to reconcile the existence of individual selves with the all-embracing character of the Absolute.

[18] By "mind-independent" is meant that the universe gives no evidence of its being mind or the experience of mind. It does not mean that the universe is not experienced as the product of mind.

us to its defects. No theory of philosophy or life can win our assent which is grounded on fallacious arguments, and it would seem that the arguments to which absolutistic idealism appeals cannot survive intellectual analysis.[19]

[19] The works of the neo-realists and the critical results may be consulted for a further criticism of objective idealism. Pragmatists may also be read with profit. The best criticism in English from a scholastic standpoint is Walker's *Theories of Knowledge*.

CHAPTER XII

OUR KNOWLEDGE OF THE WORLD

THE unreflecting man is a realist. He believes that an extramental world exists, and that he can, and does, have accurate and valid knowledge of that world. He is constantly making judgments of whose truth he is certain about the nature and qualities of the world. In his judgments he attributes qualities to things as, for example, when he affirms that things are hard, colored, or extended, and he attributes natures or essences to things, as when he classifies realities as trees, animals, gold, etc. But his convictions are spontaneous. The task devolves upon epistemology of testing these convictions to see if they can be justified by critical reflection. Can we have philosophic certitude for our spontaneous belief that through sensation we became aware of the nature and qualities of the extramental world? Can we know not only that the world exists but can we know something about it? As we might suspect there are many schools of thought which hold that the spontaneous judgments of men on this point cannot be justified.

The skeptics say the question is unanswerable. The Kantians maintain that the world exists since it is the cause of our sensations, but that in itself it is unknowable. The phenomenalist and the positivists believe that all we can know are the phenomena or reality as presented to consciousness, since nothing exists except phenomena.[1] Some of the

[1] Phenomenalism designates two different schools of thought. It is applied to the Kantian theory that all knowledge is limited to the

pragmatists say that while the knowledge of the world cannot be philosophically justified, usefulness prompts us to accept the realistic view.[2]

In opposition to these schools of thought epistemological realism maintains that it is philosophically certain that at least some of our judgments concerning the extramental world are valid and true.

There are some thinkers, styled metaphysical agnostics, who admit that we can know that reality exists, but who deny that we can know anything of the nature of reality.[3]

They contrast the process of knowledge with the object of knowledge and conclude that knowledge does not give us a true report of reality but that it transforms reality. Reality as it is in itself is different from its representation in the mind and hence is unknowable. This view is inconsistent. One cannot affirm that there is a reality which is the cause of mental appearances and hold at the same time that it is unknowable, since our saying what is not involves, in a measure, our saying what it is. If we cannot know reality we cannot know that it is and that it is a cause. Reality is either knowable or unknowable—it cannot be both. This view is based on the so-called relativity of sensation, and we shall see that the fact of relativity does not compel us to forego a knowledge of reality.

Perceptionism and Our Knowledge of the World

The division among realists noted above as regards the question of how we become aware of external reality obtains here. Both the representationists and the perceptionists believe that we can and do know the extramental, but they

---

phenomenon. It also designates that theory which holds that phenomena alone exist; there is no thing-in-itself or reality which is not related to our consciousness. The term is used here in this sense.

[2] Poincaré, *La Science et Hypothèse*, p. 246.

[3] Spencer's transfigured realism is a type of this agnosticism.

differ as to the way in which we know it. The former hold that we know only the appearances of things, i.e., the subjective representations produced in our minds by external realities.[4] Their justification of the validity of sense perception will resolve itself into an attempt to show that a correspondence of some kind exists between the subjective representations and the realities they represent.[5]

The perceptionist faces an entirely different problem. He believes that the extramental world is given to him in perception directly and immediately. As we have seen he is in thorough accord with the findings of experience; we seem to sense reality directly. We do not first know a representation of extramental reality with which the reality must be compared if we are to validate our knowledge. We know the extramental world directly and immediately and hence our knowledge is, in certain circumstances, true. We do not have to justify the truth of knowledge since knowledge is immediate and direct. There is no problem of a comparison of a reality with a mental state for us. Knowing is the presence of a reality in our consciousness, and if a reality is present we know it. To say that we do not know what we are aware of is tantamount to affirming that we do not know what we know, and this is an equivalent denial of the fact of knowledge itself. We do not, therefore, have to justify the truth claim of knowledge. Our task is negative. We must answer the objections raised against perceptionism; we must show that they do not disprove it—that they leave the true theory of perceptionism untouched. We will also

---

[4] For an exposition of this theory see Jeannière, *op. cit.*, p. 384; also Vance, *op. cit.*, passim.

[5] This is a difficult thing to prove and representationists differ considerably in their solution of the problem of the validity of our sense knowledge. Some hold that the causes of the representations are univocal with their causes; others say that they are analogous, while others admit that we can know nothing of the causes. See Coffey's *Epistemology* for a detailed criticism of representationism in this regard.

ences. This fact is a prolific cause of the so-called erroneous sensations. The truth of the matter is that the judgment and not the sensation is wrong.[9]

(2) Since the conscious datum of the extramental object is the partial result of the functioning of the sense organs and nervous system of the percipient subject, it follows that a difference in the condition of the sensory apparatus will cause a difference in the datum. The conscious data of external reality are what they are—they are always true, if conditions are taken into account. But when the abnormal conditions of sensation are not taken into account our spontaneous judgments concerning our data may be, and often are, erroneous. In other words, our senses are trustworthy; they cannot deceive us because they do not judge or interpret reality; they merely present what, under the circumstances, they must present. For example, when looking at a stick partly immersed in water we really see it bent. We cannot see it otherwise, taking into account the structure of the eye and the fact that part of the stick is seen through the air and part of it through the different medium of water. Should the stick appear straight, then the eyesight would be defective. But should we pronounce the stick to be bent our judgment would be erroneous because we would not be making due allowance for the fact that it was seen through different media.[10]

Similarly a person who is color-blind really has the sensation of gray when looking at a red object, but he would be wrong in pronouncing it gray, since he would not be discounting his color-blindness. The same is true of the data of hallucinations, dreams, etc. They are really sensed but should the person who is conscious of them identify them

---

[9] For a detailed treatment of this consult any psychology on the difference between sensation and perception.
[10] St. Thomas, *Summa*, I, q. 17, art. 2.

with reality without adverting to the abnormal condition of his sense organs or nervous system he would be in error. We hold, therefore, that the organic condition of the perceiver may be an occasion of error, as may the abnormal condition of the external object, or the abnormal condition of the medium intervening between the perceiver and perceived, but we maintain that in themselves the senses are trustworthy.

Should it be denied that the senses are trustworthy all knowledge, sense and intellectual, would be radically deceptive, since the intellect, as we have seen, derives its data from sense knowledge. Moreover, most of the arguments which are used to disprove the validity of sense knowledge, and which derive their strength from the relativity of sense knowledge, are based ultimately on the supposition that the senses report their data faithfully; hence they are groundless. Finally, since it is upon the testimony of the senses themselves that we know we have senses, it would follow logically that if it be denied that they are trustworthy, they would not be trustworthy in reporting their own existence.[11]

Normal and Abornmal Sense Perception. We have said that the sensory apparatus of the percipient subject plays a not unimportant part in sense perception. This apparatus may be in a normal or abnormal condition. Introspection informs us that we frequently make the distinction between these two conditions. We know from past experience with illusions and deceptions that we can rely on our perceptions only when they take place under normal conditions. If abnormal conditions prevail, in case we are aware of the abnormality, we either suspend our judgments altogether,

---

[11] The relativity of sense knowledge is made known to us only through the functioning of the senses. The reports of the senses in establishing the fact of relativity are held to be valid. Then the established relativity is supposed to invalidate the worth of the reports of the senses. The inconsistency is obvious.

or we emendate them by making allowance for the abnormality. The conditions which must be present if a sensation is to be normal may be divided into: (1) conditions on the part of the perceiver; (2) on the part of the perceived reality; (3) on the part of the medium.

Conditions on the part of the perceiver. The perceiver must be in a state of physical and mental health. He must be awake and must be capable of distinguishing between a datum which comes through a sense and one which is presented by the imagination. Expectation, fear, and desire are states which are largely responsible for the production of illusions; they are fruitful sources of hallucinations, and they play havoc with our perceptions.[12]

Secondly, the sense organs must be free from any influence which would make them present the datum abnormally, e.g., color-blindness, short-sightedness, deafness. It is a fact that "the quality and intensity of a sensation are affected by the quality and intensity of other simultaneous or immediately preceding sensations." As an example of such a disturbing condition we may cite again the well-known fact that the same water will feel warm or cool according as the hand has been previously immersed in water of a lower or higher temperature.[13]

When a sense organ is not under the influence of preceding or simultaneous sensations it is said to be "neutral," and if the sensation is to be normal this condition of neutrality must be present.

Conditions on the part of the object perceived. The object perceived must be at a normal distance; it must be neither too far away from, nor too close to, the perceiving organ.

---

[12] Consult any standard psychology for a treatment of this point in detail; e.g., Maher, *op. cit.*, pp. 90, 171.

[13] It is of interest to note that this example of the relativity of sensation, as well as many other instances cited by modern psychologists, has been known for centuries. See St. Thomas, *De Anima*, lib. 2, lect. 23.

The appearance of the object must persist for a time long enough to permit a distinct perception of it, and it should not move too rapidly for accurate perception. When it is a question of a perception involving the functioning of two senses we must not trust the report of one sense alone, e.g., in estimating distance we should not base our judgment on the report of the eyes alone, but on the combined report of the sense of sight and the sense of touch.

Conditions on the part of the medium. If there is a medium involved, as is the case in the functioning of the sense of sight, normal perception demands: (1) that the medium should be normal, i.e., it should be the usual medium in which we see things—the light of the sun, or white light; (2) that the medium should be homogeneous. The stick partly immersed in the water is seen through two media and hence does not appear as when seen through one.

The fact of normal and abnormal sense perception enables us to make two inferences which will serve to bring out into clearer relief our theory of perceptionism. The first of these is that it substantiates our view as to the relativity of sensation. In every sense perception some of the qualities of the sense datum are due to the nature and structure and condition of the sense organs. If the sense organs were constructed differently from what they are, our percepts would be different. This is because we are organic beings and our sense knowledge can come to us only through the channels of sense. However this must not be construed as a defect of knowledge. Knowledge is what it is; we have a certain definite perceptive nature and this perceptive nature is our only means of getting into cognitional contact with external reality. Any theory which holds that we can escape from the necessary processes of sense knowledge and contemplate reality as it is in itself, or which holds that we have some miraculous power of getting above or beyond our ordinary means of sense knowledge must be dismissed as illusory.

A second important inference is that the fact of relativity of sense knowledge does not bar us from a knowledge of reality. In fact the data we derive from the senses are the only means we have of getting at the nature and qualities of the universe. It is true that because of the factor of relativity objects are never perceived as they are. They are sensed through a medium which, according to the current teachings of science, distorts the presentation of the object. What we perceive is a subjecto-objective something, the subjective element being the contribution of the sense organ and the nervous system, and the objective element being the contribution of the perceived object. Hence the object is not the sensed object; the latter is the former transformed or metamorphosed by the perceptive process.

But we are not unconscious of the relativity of sensation; we are aware of it and we can, therefore, make allowance for it. If we did not know that sense knowledge was relative, and if we clothed the object with all the characteristics of the sense datum then our judgments concerning its qualities would be erroneous. But the critical realist does not do this. He knows what the organic factors in sensation are, and, since he allows for them, his judgments regarding extramental objects are valid. Represent the sensed object as AB, A being the contribution of the sensory apparatus, and B being the object. We know what A is, and by subtracting it from AB we achieve a knowledge of B, the object of sensation. In a word, we attribute to the object that which the object contributes to the perception.

The Relativity of Intellectual Knowledge. Can it be held that intellectual knowledge is relative? Some have extended the concept of relativity to intellectual knowledge as well as to sense knowledge because they maintain that knowledge as such conditions the object. There is no ground for this view; the knowledge of the intellect is not relative.[14]

The relativity of sense knowledge arises from the fact that sense knowledge is attained through the functioning of sense organs; these latter have an organic structure and they function in accordance with that structure. The relativity does not arise from the mere fact that objects are known, i.e., from the mere fact of knowledge itself. This is a distinction that many thinkers overlook. Because sense knowledge is relative they hurry to the conclusion that all knowledge is relative. A more careful examination of the facts shows us that the relativity which characterizes sensation is not a mental factor, is not a factor of the knowing subject as knowing, but that it is a factor of the material instrument which is employed in perception. It is not a relativity which is the result of any mental factor or of the constitution of the mind. It is an extramental relativity arising not from the self as cognitive but from the self as organic.

The "Ego-centric Predicament." Relativists rejoin that the knowledge which we have attempted to vindicate is quite valueless since it is not a knowledge of things in themselves, i.e., it is not a knowledge of reality as standing out of, and unaffected by, the knowledge relation; it is merely a knowledge of realities within that relation, and consequently affected by it. We cannot get at the world of reality without

[14] The knowledge of the intellect is not relative in the sense in which the term is used by relativists. Knowledge is relative in the sense "(A) that we can know only as much as our faculties, limited in number and range, can reveal to us; (B) that these faculties can inform us of objects only so far, and accordingly as the latter manifest themselves; (C) that accordingly (a) there may remain always an indefinite number of qualities which we do not know, and (b) what is known must be set in relation to the mind, and can only be known in such relation. So much relativity is necessarily involved in the very nature of knowledge, but it in no way destroys the worth of that knowledge." Maher, *op. cit.*, p. 158.

experiencing it in some way. We cannot conceive a thing as existing apart from consciousness because our very conception of it brings it within our consciousness. Hence we have no right to say that our knowledge is truly representative of things as they are in themselves. This is called in modern thought the "ego-centric" predicament.[15]

It is a real predicament. But it is at best a methodological predicament. We cannot know a thing without knowing it; we cannot think of a thing without thinking of it, we cannot conceive a thing without conceiving it. To know things as they are in themselves in the ordinary understanding of that phrase is a contradiction in terms for it implies that they are known and unknown at the same time. "If knowledge is defined to imply a relation between the mind and a known object, and if the noumenon or thing-in-itself is defined to signify a real element of an object which never stands in any relation to our cognitive powers, then a knowledge of noumena or things-in-themselves is obviously an absurdity."[16]

Does the ego-centric predicament prove any thing? If the knowing of reality changes reality, if it affects the reality in some way, then known realities are clearly different from the same realities as unknown, although we cannot say in what way. However this theory refutes itself. No relativist can consistently profess this view for in so doing he is tacitly presupposing that his knowledge of the fact of relativity is not relative. Any theory which holds that the factors of

---

[15] Cf., Perry, *op. cit.*, p. 128; Spaulding, *op. cit.*, passim; Coffey, *Epist.*, Vol. II, p. 156.

[16] Maher, *op. cit.*, p. 158. "To speak of 'knowing,' 'things in themselves,' or 'things as they are,' is to talk not simply of an impossibility, but a contradiction; for these phrases are invented to denote what *is* in the sphere of *being* and *not in the sphere of thought;* and to suppose them *known* is *ipso facto* to take away this character. The relativity of cognition (i.e., in the sense defined) imposes on us no forfeiture of privilege, no humiliation of pride; there is not any conceivable form of apprehension from which it excludes us." Martineau, *A Study of Religion*, Vol. I, p. 119.

intellectual cognition fuse with, or transform, or transfigure the presentment of reality to the mind is self-contradictory. It denies that we can have absolute truth about anything and yet it sets up its own theory as absolutely true, i.e., as giving the true state of affairs as regards the nature of knowledge. On its own premises it is quite without value. Epitomizing our doctrine on relativity—*perceptual knowledge is relative, but intellectual knowledge is not relative.*

CHAPTER XIII

OBJECTIONS TO PERCEPTIONISM. DIFFICULTIES OF REALISM

A PLAUSIBLE objection has been raised against the basic principle of perceptionism, viz., directness of external perception, and its plausibility has been the main support of representationism and idealism. This objection takes the form of a denial of the fact of direct external perception. It may be stated thus: that of which we are immediately and directly aware in sense perception cannot be the physical objects of the extramental world since, if this were the case, contradictory predicates would belong to these objects. But the physical sciences show that this latter conclusion is absurd. Hence what we perceive, what we are directly and immediately aware of in sense perception is not the object but a mental representation or "appearance" of the object. The impossibility of identifying physical things with sense data is readily apparent when we consider the spatial and temporal characters of sense data and physical objects respectively. It is a commonplace of our experience that as objects move further and further away from us their sense data become smaller, e.g., a man walking away from us becomes smaller and smaller until he dwindles to a mere speck on the horizon. Now science will not permit us to suppose that his body actually diminishes in size; neither will the experience of the man himself. But since what we perceive does diminish in size, since there is a series of differences in the data to which there correspond no differences in the object represented by the data, the two cannot be identical. In other words, unless we are willing to grant the apparently absurd conclusion that an object can be large and small at the same time, unless we grant that it can have contradictory characteristics, we must admit that what we perceive is not the object but a presentment, or a representation, or a mental appearance, of the object.[1]

The disparity between the object of perception and the real object becomes more apparent when we view the temporal relations between the two. The varying distance of objects from us involves a difference in the time it takes them to produce an impression in us. Ordinarily the object of our perception and the real object exist simultaneously. But it may happen that the physical object has ceased to exist when we are perceiving what we identify with it. Astronomers tells us that a star we now perceive has been destroyed centuries ago—so long does it take light to travel from it to us. And theoretically our percept of falling snow flakes and the snow flakes themselves have not temporal coincidence. This lack of temporal coincidence between the percept and the object of the percept clearly points to the fact that the object of perception is not the real object, that what we perceive is not the object but a mental something which is the effect of the object on our perceptive organism.[2]

CRITICISM: The facts adduced above do not invalidate the contention that we perceive things and not their representa-

---

[1] Other examples of contradictory attributes commonly used by the opponents of perceptionism are: Tepid water is hot to the cold hand and cold to the hot hand—it is hot and non-hot; a coin revolved on its axis is round and elliptical or non-round; railroad tracks converge in the distance—they are parallel and non-parallel; colors of things vary with their distance from the perceiver and with different perceivers. See Jeannière, *op. cit.*, p. 398; Russell, *Problems of Philosophy*, p. 15; Fullerton, *An Introduction to Philosophy*, p. 60; Vance, *op. cit.*, chap. 1.

[2] *Essays in Critical Realism*, Drake et al., p. 226.

tions. These facts can be harmonized with the theory of perceptionism. We account for the varying presentation of the object by the relativity of sensation. We do not claim that perceptionism involves our always perceiving the object the same. The fact that we perceive through our senses forbids this. Our perception is conditioned by the functioning of the sense organs. In the case of vision, for example, we can only see as the eyes permit us to see. Whenever the eyes are used we see things according to the laws of perspective. We cannot help seeing things in this way as it is a necessary condition of vision. Things at a distance from us necessarily appear smaller than these same things when viewed nearer to us. But whether they are near to us or distant from us it is the objects we sense and not their mental representations. There is therefore no contradiction between admitting that the appearances of things differ and holding that we perceive the object and not its appearance. Our perception of the object may change but all the time it is the perception *of* the object.

As regards contradictory predicates being true simultaneously of the same object, we reply that a thing perceived under the same conditions, subjective and objective, will not be perceived in different ways. The fact of the relativity of sensation makes this objection irrelevant. An object seen at various distances from the perceiver does and must appear to be of different sizes. But the same object seen under exactly the same conditions will not give rise to different mental presentments. The view that it is the object we perceive, whether it be near or far, is in no way incompatible with the fact of relativity.

Similarly the lack of temporal coincidence between the object and its representation is not apposite to a theory of perceptionism which takes account of the relativity of sensation. In seeing objects we are dependent on light waves which come from the object to our eyes. The light waves are an essential element in vision, so much so that without them there is no vision. And since these waves are not instantaneous in traversing space it is clear that sometimes there will be a lack of temporal coincidence between our perception of the object and the object itself. But while this cannot be avoided since it is essential in the seeing process, it in no way impugns our claim that it is the object we see and not a mental modification caused by the object. In the case mentioned above, of the stars which have disappeared and which are still seen, they are still cognitionally present. In order for a thing to be seen it must be presented to the eye—it must be in the field of vision. Owing to the immense distance between our eyes and the place where the stars were, and because of the relatively long time it takes the light waves to traverse that distance, they are still in the field of vision—they are really perceptually present to us, and we see them although they have disappeared.[3]

It cannot be too strongly stressed that the tendency of philosophers of an idealistic bent to erect between the mind and reality a barrier of appearances or mental representations which are known immediately, and which serve as a medium through which we acquire a knowledge of the extramental world, is based on a confusion of the process of knowledge with the object of knowledge. Perception on the subjective side is a process whereby a mind perceives an object. Looked at objectively it is a process whereby an object appears to, or is presented to, a mind. The knowledge-process is not that which we perceive; it is that by which we perceive. If the process is identified with the object of knowledge there must be introduced between the mind and the object subsidiary mental entities, appearances, and the like, to close

[3] Fullerton, *The World We Live In*, p. 157.

the gap between the mind and the object. But this introduction is not only unnecessary—it is erroneous; it results in a misstating of the problem of the truth-value of sensation, and a consequent rendering of the problem insoluble from a realistic standpoint. Perceptionism admits the existence of these mental states but it insists that they are not objects of knowledge, and it thus escapes the confusion which vitiates a great deal of modern thought.

Objections against Realism

Sense Illusions. The existence of sense illusions is utilized as an argument against realism. By illusions are meant mistaken mental constructs which have apparently reliable data for their basis. When these data are furnished by the senses they are called sense illusions. Illusions occur in connection with all the senses. The "moving" picture is an instance of an optical illusion. The eyes perceive the pictures on the screen as "moving" whereas in reality they are at rest—the illusion of movement being due to the fact that each picture remains on the screen longer than the time taken for the transition from picture to picture. The latter interval is so brief that the real movement of picture succeeding picture is imperceptible, while the pictures at rest are clearly perceived.[4]

It is argued that since illusions are a fact the senses are sometimes in error when they report extramental reality to us. They are not, therefore, reliable guides to a knowledge of reality.

Sense illusions are due either to subjective or objective conditions. The senses must present things as they do; they cannot do otherwise, the conditions under which sensations

---

[4] Consult any standard psychology for other optical, tactile, and muscular illusions.

occur being taken into account. Hence we cannot have a "false" sensation or an "illusion" in the strict sense of those terms. Our judgments based on the data of sensations may be false because sometimes the subjective and objective conditions under which sensations occur are not adverted to. But we can by reflection discover when the conditions are abnormal, and we can make allowance for the abnormality, in which case we will not be the victim of the illusion. The fact that there are illusions has a practical import. It shows us that we must not make hurried or uncritical judgments; we should always assiduously scrutinize the conditions under which our sensations occur.

Another objection against the reliability of the senses is: vibrations of the ether (or air) are utterly unlike our sensations of color and sound, and yet what we see and hear are vibrations of the ether (in the case of vision) or air (in the case of hearing). Hence our senses are not reliable in reporting the nature of reality. This objection can be summarily dealt with. We learned of the existence of ether and air vibrations through the data given to the senses. Scientists established their theories of color and sound on facts furnished by sense knowledge. Hence if these theories of science are true they prove, if anything, that the senses are trustworthy sources of information about the extramental order.

The Subjectivity or Objectivity of Sense Qualities. To what extent do sense qualities belong to objects? Is grass really green, or is greenness a property only of the energy of the stimulus of the grass as modified by the optic nerve and the brain? The question is unanswerable because science has not told us what alteration the energy of the stimulus undergoes in passing through the optic nerve and the brain. If we knew this we would know something of the difference between objective and subjective aspects of sense qualities. If the energies of the brain and ocular apparatus were the same as the vibrations of a seen body we could conclude that color was an intrinsic quality of a body—that grass was really green. The optic nerve is, however, a very different kind of medium from the ether, and hence it may be that the energy is changed somewhat in its passage through the nerve. And yet recent experiments have shown that this change is not as great as has been thought.[5]

Until science comes to our rescue with the empirical solution of this question we cannot answer.

A very common question is: Are sense qualities in unperceived reality at all? If so, in what way are they present? Have flowers color if no one is looking at them? Are stones hard when no one is touching them? We believe that sense qualities are in unperceived reality potentially or virtually, i.e., given the proper circumstances they will be perceived; they will give rise to the sensations of color, taste, resistance, etc. Untasted sugar has real sweetness, but not the taste of sweetness (or perceived sweetness). In the unseen rose there is color, but not the vision of color (or perceived color). In unheard winds there is real sound, but not the hearing of sound (or perceived sound). In other words, if by "taste," "color," "sound," etc., we mean the actual perception of these qualities then these qualities are not in the domain of external reality, since perception is not objective but subjective. But if by these terms we mean qualities which will give rise in normal perception to the corresponding perceptions of "taste," etc., then these qualities are objective and real. It is to be noted that this distinction between the mental and physical aspects of sense qualities is not a discovery of modern thought. We find it mentioned by

[5] *The New Realism*, p. 397.

Aristotle.[6] In fact he drew attention to the ambiguity arising from the use of the same word (taste, sound, color) to designate both the unperceived and the perceived physical property. St. Thomas also comments on the same fact.[7]

[6] *De Anima,* lib. 3, lect. 2.
[7] *Comm. de Anima,* lib., 3, 1, 2, ad finem.

CHAPTER XIV

TWO CONTEMPORARY AMERICAN THEORIES OF REALISM. NEO-REALISM AND CRITICAL REALISM

MODERN realism did not originate until the dawn of the twentieth century. William James had previously inveighed with vigor against Hegelian idealism but he did not meet with much encouragement. The older philosophy was too strongly entrenched. In Germany the cause of realism was first espoused by Husserl who published his monumental work, *Logische Untersuchungen,* in 1900. The realistic movement received added impact from the works of Meinong who published his *Ueber Annahmen* in 1902 and his *Gegandstandstheorie und Psychologie* in 1904.[1]

In England G. E. Moore and Bertrand Russell were the pioneers of the new movement. Moore fired the opening gun in a crusade for realistic thought in his essay, "The Refutation of Idealism." [2]

Russell's *Principles of Mathematics* was a plea for the realistic position, as were his later works, *Our Knowledge of the External World* and *The Problems of Philosophy.*[3]

The American swing toward realism followed shortly afterwards. Idealism of the German and English type had long held the field in this country. James' preachment of

---

[1] Both these philosophers were probably influenced by the scholastic views of Brentano (d. 1917).
[2] See "Mind," N.S., 1903; this essay is contained in his *Philosophical Studies,* 1922.
[3] These works were published in 1903, 1914 and 1912 respectively. Russell's thought has changed much since his initial adoption of realism.

realism was the result of a psychological approach to the problem of knowledge. He interpreted mind to be a relation between objects which existed in their own right. He professed a "radical empiricism," the essence of which was that reality was given immediately, and that the difference between the physical and the mental was, therefore, merely a relational difference or a difference of perspective.

NEO-REALISM —

During the first years of this century a younger group of philosophers undertook an analysis of the problem of knowledge from the realistic standpoint. Their thought was essentially a protest against the basic tenets of objective idealism. They agreed that the mind does not constitute reality but that it apprehends reality. They maintained against all forms of mediate or representationistic realism that physical existents are as immediately present to the perceiving subject as are logical existents to thought. Their denial of the intercalation of mental representations between the object and the mind resulted in a form of epistemological monism. The physical organism of the knower reacts to certain selected parts of his environment and through this reaction these parts of the environment are made the content of the knowledge of the organism. Knowledge is nothing but givenness; physical facts are numerically identical with percepts (or concepts). In becoming the content of a subject's awareness these facts simply received a special grouping, a new connection, because of their new relation with the reacting organism. The knowledge of an object is simply a new and external, but temporary, relation into which the object has entered. Since neither the existence nor the nature of an object depends on its being known, the knowledge-relation is external. In fact relations are real and independent of each other; they do not constitute reality. This school is opposed to anti-intellectualism and it submits that logical analysis is the correct method to be followed by the epistemologist.

As regards their ontology the neo-realists agree in predicating to objects an existence which is neither physical nor psychical but which is "neutral." Psychologically they tend to behaviorism in their conception of mind in terms of reaction to an environment, and in their belief that consciousness is neither absolutely private nor subjective. They are opposed to the category of substance in both the physical and mental fields, substituting for it the category of function. The chief exponents of this school published a cooperative volume, *The New Realism,* in 1912. They have many points of contact but their later writings show that their divergences are being widened.[4]

CRITICISM: *The neo-realistic theory of mind.* A detailed discussion of the neo-realistic view of the nature of consciousness belongs to psychology, but it will not be out of place to point out briefly that this conception of consciousness can find no basis in experience. When I see the color of this book it is not the color of the book that is conscious. And when I see that the color of the book is different from the color of grass, the principle of difference is not conscious. *I* am conscious of the color of the book, of the color of the grass, and of the difference in color between the book and the grass. The fact is that I have a consciousness and that my consciousness is mine—it is not a consciousness residing in the realities I sense.

The neo-realist neglects the fact of "giveness."[5] He has not distinguished between the existence of a thing and its appearance. An object may exist without appearing but

[4] See Holt, *The Concept of Consciousness;* Montague, *The Ways of Knowing;* Perry, *Present Philosophical Tendencies; The Present Conflict of Ideals; General Theory of Value;* Spaulding, *The New Rationalism.*
[5] See Strong, *The Origin of Consciousness,* p. 31.

it is difficult to see how it can appear unless it appears to something, or unless there is an awareness of it. It cannot appear to another reality unless this latter is conscious of it. The fact that objects are given always implies that there is a "giveness." The neo-realistic theory of consciousness is seemingly a theory of the objects of consciousness and not a theory of consciousness at all. The attempt to split up the conscious state that intervenes between the knower and the object of his knowledge into an "act" and a "content" founders on the rock of fact. Introspection indisputably shows us that we have mental states, and that these are not identical with objects of the physical or logical orders. The neo-realist must admit that he is conscious of his theory of consciousness—despite the paradox that his theory of consciousness denies that he is conscious.[6]

Neo-realism and the physiology of perception. Science informs us that the physical object which initiates the perceptive process from the objective side is not identical with the percept which it engenders. How can the object of a percept and the percept be identified? Between them there intervenes the series of physical and psychical events enumerated above.[7]

The sensation is not identical with its cause, and the sensed object is not identical with its effect. The facts are clearly against this tenet of neo-realism. The facts noted in connection with the relativity of sensation cannot be reconciled with the neo-realistic hypothesis. How can the various visual images, for example, which different observers derive from the same object be identified with the single object sensed.

Neo-realism and the privacy of minds. Selfhood is a

---

[6] See Lovejoy, "The Paradox of the Thinking Behaviorist," *Phil. Review*, XXXI, p. 141; confer also Turner, *A Theory of Direct Realism*, chap. 12.
[7] See p. 138.

patent fact. The nature of the self may be disputed but the fact of selfhood is indisputable. Our selves are unique existences which are impervious to other selves; they are individual, private and personal. Nothing seems to be plainer than this, and yet the neo-realist is compelled to hold that the content of one mind may be numerically identical with the content of other minds. Your feelings, emotions, pains, and thoughts may be numerically one with mine. He not only maintains that I can know *about* your thoughts but that my thoughts *are* your thoughts. The contents of our thoughts may, of course, be similar, i.e., we may think about the same things, but the existence of our thoughts as psychological phenomena or entities in different centers of consciousness forbids their being numerically identified. The breaches between "thoughts belonging to different personal minds . . . are the most absolute breaches in nature." [8]

If the neo-realistic identification of the subjective with the objective has any plausibility it is in the instance of veridical ideas. But as regards other subjective states their contention lacks all plausibility. In fact it is difficult to understand how the subjectivity and privacy of our ideas of non-existent beings, such as round circles, of our emotions, of our pains, of our awareness of meaning, can be denied.

Neo-realism and error. The existence of error is a fact admitted by all theories of knowledge. It must therefore be explained by them. They must prove that knowledge can be true and that it may be false. Neo-realism has proved that knowledge can be true. But it has gone further—it has seemingly proved that knowledge must be true. If knowledge is what neo-realism affirms it to be it is difficult to see how the mind can fall into error. The elimination of sensations and ideas from the knowledge process has apparently eliminated the possibility of error. The possibility of error

[8] James, *Psychology*, p. 153.

seems to demand a clear-cut distinction between the physical and the psychical in the formation of knowledge.[9]

Critical Realism

Critical realism emerged simultaneously with neo-realism but it did not present its platform to the thinking world until 1920 when Drake, Lovejoy, Pratt, Rogers, Santayana, Sellars, and Strong, coöperated in publishing *Essays in Critical Realism*.[10]

There is a sharp cleavage between the critical and the neo-realists. Negatively both schools reject idealism root and branch, but positively neo-realism is an epistemological monism while critical realism is an epistemological dualism. The latter does not believe that the attempt of the former to bridge the subject-object gap is successful. The facts do not permit us to hold that objects are actually present in consciousness. Perception is not a two-term relation. The difference between the two schools results ultimately from their different views on the nature of consciousness. For the neo-realist consciousness, in the traditional sense of that term, does not exist. There is no need for consciousness if by the latter is meant a special kind of reality which is psychic in nature. The psychic is really the physical in new relations.

The critical realist, on the contrary, regards consciousness as an interpretative function of the organism to which it belongs. It is not the object to which the organism is react-

---

[9] For other criticisms of neo-realism consult, *Essays in Critical Realism*. Evans, *New Realism and Old Reality*, is a critique of this system from an idealistic standpoint; it contains a good bibliography. The best critique of neo-realism from a neo-scholastic standpoint is Kremer's *Le néo-réalisme américain*.

[10] See also Drake, *Mind and Its Place in Nature;* Pratt, *Matter and Spirit;* Sellars, *Critical Realism; Evolutionary Naturalism;* Strong, *A Theory of Knowledge; The Origin of Consciousness;* Santayana, *The Life of Reason, Winds of Doctrine, Scepticism and Animal Faith; The Realm of Essence*.

ing at any given time. It has an intraorganic realm of its own. Its states are not the objects of its states—as the neo-realist holds. Knowledge for the critical realist is not mere "giveness"—it is rather an interpretation of a selected object by means of characters discriminated in the field of consciousness.

The critical realist is of the opinion that knowledge of extramental reality is constituted of three terms—the mind, the object, and the datum. He rejects idealism and representative realism because these theories maintain that the data of our perceptions are but psychological existents. Neither of these theories, he holds, is able to vindicate the truth of knowledge. Furthermore they are both psychologically false. Our data cannot be our mental states; the qualities of the data and of our mental states are too disparate to permit such an identification.[11] Furthermore if two persons perceive the same datum the mental state of one, simply because it is his, must differ qualitatively from the mental state of the other.

Neither can the physical object be the datum. Hence a true theory of perception must take into account the three elements, object, mind, and datum, none of which are reducible to the others.

What is the datum, and what is the part it plays in perception? The answer to these questions brings out the essential character of critical realism in distinction from other realistic theories. The datum is the essence (or character-complex) which through perception is taken to be a character of the perceived object. The latter causes the appearance of certain character-complexes in the percipient subject. These character complexes are the data—the objects of awareness in the percipient subject—which are projected by the subject into the extramental world, or which are imagined to be in

[11] See *Essays in Critical Realism*, p. 223.

the objective world. When the perception is true these data are identical with the characteristics of the perceived object. Hence in a true perception the data (or character-complexes) are actual characteristics of the object which caused their perception in the mind. In a false perception this identity is lacking, and the status of the data is subjective, i.e., they are but subjective phenomena.

Do these essences exist? They do not exist as ontological entities; they are rather logical subsistences. But as logical subsistences their subsistence does not depend on their being known. Santayana avers that essences are immutable and intrinsic; they exist in the universe awaiting discovery by our minds. They represent the whatness or nature of objects and hence when the mind apprehends them it knows reality in a very real sense. Briefly, critical realism submits that since we know the qualities of an object through its data which are given to us we know the object. The object itself, however, regarded as a physical existent, the "that" as distinguished from the "what," cannot be perceived by us.[12]

CRITICISM: As has been indicated, critical realism differs from neo-realism in its belief that the knowledge process is three-termed, consisting of the conscious organism, the object known, and the datum or character-complex. The introduction of the latter has enabled this school to evade many of the difficulties of neo-realism. But it is on this doctrine of the datum that their critics have centered their attack. The criticisms directed against the datum fall into two main classes.

(1) The datum prevents the knowledge of reality. If the mind can cognize the datum alone, and if it can never

[12] The critical realists are by no means unanimous in the detailed exposition of their system. Some approximate idealism while others are ultra-realistic. The above account of their system is an attempt to outline the points on which they agree.

attain the object known, it seems to follow logically that the mind can never achieve a knowledge of reality.

This dilemma faces Critical Realism. If it maintains its universal distinction between physical things themselves beyond our consciousness, and their perceived or apparent sense-characters, then it becomes a noumenalism. But if on the other hand it founds its affirmations on instinctive belief, it forfeits all title to be regarded as a philosophical system, whatever merits it may possess. Or at best it can become a philosophy only of the content of perception as distinct from physical reality itself.[13]

If this charge is true it follows that on the tenets of this theory we cannot know that reality exists or that it can produce a datum in our minds. Neither can we know that the datum (if it exists) is a valid representation of the reality of which it is the datum. The validity of our knowledge will thus of necessity always be conjectural. Critical realism, it is alleged, cannot provide us with a criterion for testing the truth of our knowledge; if our knowledge is true we can never prove it to be true.

(2) The datum is the result of the influence of the known object on the conscious organism. If the known object does not influence the mind there can be no datum. Yet knowledge is sometimes erroneous. How can erroneous data be presented to the mind? Not by the objects perceived since they can only present true data; data must be presentments of objects. Once it is admitted that data do not come from objects then it must also be admitted that our minds can themselves generate data—data which do not derive from objects—and in that event why assume that any data come from objects?

The theory of critical realism is not easily understood. One

[13] Turner, *op. cit.*, p. 129; the whole of chapter nine of this work can be read with profit; consult also Bosanquet, *The Meeting of Extremes in Contemporary Philosophy*, p. 127.

of the chief impediments to a clear understanding of this theory is the divergences that separate its adherents, and the consequent lack of harmony in their realistic *credos*. To epistemologistical dualists critical realism seems to be an onward step toward the solution of the knowledge-problem. At least it can be said to be without the insuperable difficulties that encumber neo-realism and all forms of epistemological monism.

It may be that some of the critics of this school have not fully envisaged its essential doctrine. There is some excuse for this because of the conflicting statements of its proponents. For instance, we are told that "what we perceive . . . is the outer object itself," and "we directly perceive . . . the character of objects." [14]

But we are also told that "the physical thing and the psychic state. . . unquestionably two and mutually independent. . . . The knower is confined to the datum, and can never literally inspect the existent. . . . We have no power of penetrating to the object itself and intuiting it immediately." [15]

Again we are informed, "Characteristics appear to us; objects themselves do not get within our consciousness; the physical existent itself does not get within experience; knowledge is a beholding of its nature." [16]

If these and other apparently conflicting passages may be interpreted to mean that the physical existent does not enter consciousness as such, i.e., that it does not enter our consciousness physically or as a physical object, but that it enters our consciousness cognitively by means of our perceptions, then critical reason seemingly escapes the charge of being a form of representative realism. If our perceptions

---

[14] *Essays in C. R.*, p. 4; p. 24.
[15] *Ibidem*, pp. 203, 225, 240.
[16] *Ibidem*, p. 26; see also pp. 29 and 196.

are perceptions of reality then our knowledge may be said to be direct. If the data are means whereby we are made aware of reality, and this is not unreasonable since data are data of reality, then knowledge is immediate in a real sense. But will all the critical realists subscribe to these statements?

Again, essences are not logical entities floating in some vague way between the object and the mind. The conception that the essence or whatness of an object leaves the object and enters into the mind is quite impossible. Essences can perform no such feats. The intellect guided by the presentment of the object forms the concept of the essence of the object. Here again the intellectual conception of the essence of the object is immediate and direct. The known or conceptual essence is the essense of the object represented in the mind.

If critical realism can avoid the confusion referred to above, viz., the confusion of the process of thought with the object of thought, it will escape many of the censures directed against it.

CHAPTER XV

TRUTH

The question of the truth of knowledge cannot be answered until we know what truth is. What does the word "truth" mean? What do we mean by saying that a judgment is true, or by declaring that another judgment is false? More concretely, what do I mean when I say that the judgment, "Washington is in the District of Columbia" is true, and that the judgment, "Washington is in California" is false? What is the truth about truth?

There are three dominant theories of truth, the correspondence theory, the coherence theory, and the pragmatic theory.

The Correspondence Theory

We use the word "truth" in three ways—we apply it to things, to speech, and to thought. Thus we say, "He is a true friend," meaning that this person (he) conforms to my idea of what a friend is. This is an instance of ontological truth or the truth of things. Again we say, "He tells the truth," or, "He is truthful." We mean that the words used by the person spoken of are a faithful expression of what is in his mind; they are conformed to, or represent what he thinks. This is an instance of moral truth, or the truth of language. Again we say, "His views are true," meaning thereby that his views represent faithfully, or conform to, the matter about which the views are entertained.

This is an instance of logical truth, or the truth of thought, and it is this which concerns the epistemologist. It must be noted that in all three kinds of truth there is the common element of conformity.[1]

<u>*Ontological Truth.*</u> This species of truth may be defined as the conformity between two thought-objects, one of which is, or has been, perceived, and the other which is a preconceived mental type. We compare an object with another term, viz., the type which we conceive as realizing the definition of the object. The first term of the comparison, the object present here and now (or remembered), is given through experience, while the second is an abstract concept already in the mind. When the first coincides or conforms with the second we say that it is truly the second, or that it is the second. For example I have a concept of what constitutes an American. He possesses certain qualities which distinguish him from other men, and which characterize him alone. I meet a man who has these same qualities and I say, "He is a true American," or "He is an American," thereby asserting an identity between the person perceived and the type already conceived in my mind. Hence ontological truth may be defined as "the conformity (or adequation) of a thing with the intellect." This is the traditional scholastic definition of ontological truth, but it must be born in mind that, if it is to be of value, "thing" means an object perceived or imagined, and "intellect" means the preconceived abstract type. The conformity of the object perceived with the mental type is the truth of the object, and for this reason ontological truth is said to be objective or the truth of objects.[2] All things are ontologically true in the sense that they conform to and embody ideas in the mind of God.

[1] St. Thomas, *Summa,* I, XXI, art. 2.
[2] Usually in judgments having to do with the truth of objects we use the words "original," "genuine," "real," "faithful," etc., instead of "true," e.g., "This is an original Corot," "This is real wool."

168 ELEMENTS OF EPISTEMOLOGY

They are also ontologically true inasmuch as they have the power of engendering in our minds ideas which represent them faithfully.

Logical Truth. Logical truth is the conformity or adequation of the intellect with the thing.³

It is the conformity of the mind judging about reality, or of the mind's judgment about reality, with the reality to which the judgment refers.⁴

"The truth of the intellect is the adequation of the thing and the intellect, in such a way that the intellect says that is which is, and that is not which is not." ⁵

To avoid prevalent misconceptions of this definition it must be noted that:

(1) The conformity in question is *sui generis*. It is not a physical conformity; neither is it photographic. We deprecate the crude "copy" theory of correspondence. A judgment does not picture the reality about which it is made as a mirror pictures the image of an object placed before it. The conformity is mental or intentional.⁶

(2) The conformity is not adequate, i.e., it does not represent all the notes of the object. It is a partial conformity. This does not mean, however, that because it is partial it is untrue. It is true if the note expressed by the judgment as belonging to the object is in the object in reality.

(3) When it is said that the conformity is of the "intellect" we mean by the latter term the intellect as judging. Truth or falsity can be attributed only to judgments. If a judgment is true it follows that the concepts or percepts of which it is made up are also true. But the latter are true only inchoatively, i.e., in as much as there is a conformity

---

³ St. Thomas, *Summa*, I, XXI, art. 2.
⁴ Coffey, *Science of Logic*, Vol. II, p. 210.
⁵ St. Thomas, *Contra Gentiles*, I, q. 5.
⁶ See Rickaby, *First Principles of Knowledge*, p. 4; Maher, *op. cit.*, p. 52.

between them and the reality they represent. It is only in judgments that the objectivity of ideas is asserted and hence they alone can be said to be true or false.[7]

(4) The term "thing" (or reality) means: (a) Any possible or any real thing, whether in the subjective or objective order. (b) A thing not as it is in itself, standing out of all relation to the mind, and independent of the mind, but a thing as represented to the mind. It is obviously a contradiction in terms to speak of knowing things which are not related to the mind, or which are not present to the mind.

(5) When the mind makes a judgment it pronounces two distinct concepts (or percepts), the subject and the predicate of the judgment, to be objectively and really identical, if the judgment is affirmative, or objectively and really non-identical, if the judgment is negative. A judgment is true when the verdict of the mind is in accord with the relation between the realities represented by the concepts (or percepts). In other words, a judgment is true when it attributes to its subject a nature or quality which *de facto* belongs to it. To judge things are what they are is to judge truly. If, on the contrary, the mind asserts that a relation exists between the subject and predicate which does not exist objectively, if it asserts that the subject has a nature or quality which in reality does not belong to it, the judgment is false.

Objections to the Correspondence Theory

The critics of this theory are legion—as are their objections to it. We shall cite but two of the latter. It is said that in this theory both terms of the truth relation are subjective, and that there is no conformity, therefore, of the "intellect" with the "thing." This objection is due to a misapprehension. One term of the relation is subjective, viz., the mental state

[7] St. Thomas, *Summa,* I, 16, 2.

which is the result of the judgment, or of the interpretation of the object presented to the mind. But the other term is not subjective since it is the extramental reality which is presented to the mind. When the reality is presented to the mind it acquires an ideal existence in the mind, otherwise it could not be known. But it is not this latter that is the term to which we conform our judgments. It is not an object of knowledge at all. It is simply the means whereby we become aware of the reality in question, and it is the reality of which we are aware to which we conform our judgments. Hence there is a real conformity of our judgments with reality.[8]

The second objection is the stock objection against the correspondence theory. If truth is a conformity between a judgment and the reality judged about, then it is and must be unknowable. How can we ever discover whether or not our judgments represent reality as it really is? We can never know when we possess the truth because we can never check up our judgments with reality as it is in itself, i.e., as unknown. We can tell whether a photograph is good or bad only by comparing it with its original. But in the case of knowledge we can get at the original only by knowing it, which means that the thing as it is in itself, and with which we must compare our judgments if we are to validate them, can never be attained.

This theory of truth involves no such absurdity. We grant that it is impossible to compare our judgments with realities which are not present to our minds, since it is only by means of thought that things are known. We claim no second sight or telepathic vision by means of which we can detect the agreement or disagreement of an unknown reality with its mental representation. But while truth is a correspond-

[8] Coffey, *Epist.*, Vol. II, p. 253.

ence, this correspondence can be known if we can know that the judgment has been determined by reality. When, on reflection, we find a discrepancy between our thought and the evidence of reality—which evidence is nothing but the presentment of the reality to the mind—then we know we are in error; but when we find an agreement between our judgment and reality, when we find our judgment is in accord with the evidence, then we know we possess the truth.

Can we ever know that our judgments have been determined by reality? It would seem that we can. The data of our experience do not explain of themselves their existence in our minds. What we experience is due to the action of reality upon our minds. Because of this fact we can learn something of the world which is acting upon us. On the basis of our perceptual data we construct conceptual theories about the world, theories which explain the nature of the world, and between which and the world they seek to explain, there exists a conformity, if they are true. We cannot compare the world as unknown with these theories, but we can, and do, test the truth of these theories by the success or failure of the expectations we base upon them.

Science elaborates a theory concerning some aspect of the physical universe. That theory cannot be compared with the physical objects in question as they stand out of all relation to the mind. But if the theory is true it must explain the behavior of these physical objects. If in a particular situation these objects do not act in accord with the tenets of the theory, the theory is judged to be false. If, on the contrary, in all observable instances the behavior of the realities in question is what we would expect it to be, the theory is true. And it is true because it conforms to reality—things are what the theory claims them to be. The correspondence theory of truth is, therefore, "not affected by the specious objection that it is impossible for us to discover agreements or disagreements between experiential effects and the extra-experiential causes of these effects. What we cannot directly observe we can indirectly infer." [9]

The Coherence Theory

This is the theory proposed by objective idealism. Since in that system there is no reality to which judgments can conform—thought and reality being identified—idealists are forced to make truth an internal characteristic of judgments themselves. The ultimate criterion of truth is the mutual coherence or harmonious organization of judgments into a system. A single judgment is true only in so far as it fits into the completely articulated system of truths. "Truth, in its essential nature, is that systematic coherence which is the character of a significant whole." [10]

CRITICISM: (1) This theory stands or falls with objective idealism. We believe that objective idealism is not true, and in that event this theory is false.

(2) The test of coherence is impracticable. We cannot know the totality of truth and hence we cannot use this criterion to determine the truth of our individual judgments. I am certain of a great many truths, truths of the real order and truths of the ideal order, I am certain of historical facts, but I do not know how these convictions enter into the whole of truth. I believe that all true judgments cohere but I do not know what particular place any one judgment may occupy in the whole. The coherence theory while expressing

---

[9] Montague, *op. cit.*, p. 260; consult also Walker, *op. cit.*, and Coffey, *Epist.*; Roger's *What Is Truth?* is an exposition of the correspondence theory.

[10] Joachim, *The Nature of Truth*, p. 76. This work and Bosanquet's *Logic*, Vol. II, chaps. 9-10, and *The Principle of Individuality and Value* are perhaps the best exposition of the coherence theory.

an ideal that controls thought, does not afford us a working criterion.

(3) Coherence is but a negative test of truth. It is possible to construct systems of thought which are coherent, each part being perfectly articulated into every other part, and yet the whole structure might be false. All true judgments are coherent, but not all coherent judgments are true.

(4) The coherence theory is self-contradictory. Idealism extends its modification theory of relations to truth, holding that any one single truth is true only by virtue of its relations to all other truths. It follows that we can never know one truth unless we know all the other truths to which it is related. Only an infinite mind can know all truth and the relationships between single truths, and hence only an infinite mind can achieve absolute truth. In the face of this theory idealists, men of finite minds, put forth the single truth of their theory which they hold is absolutely true. In so doing they conflict with their own theory of truth in a threefold way: (a) in as much as they are finite; (b) in as much as they put forth their theory which is a single truth; (c) in so far as they put it forth as absolutely true. They cannot maintain this theory with contradicting its presuppositions. If no judgment is wholly true to a finite mind then the judgment that truth is coherence is not wholly true to a finite mind.[11]

(5) Some idealists hold that theories are true, not so much because of their coherence with the rest of knowledge, but because their parts are consistent with each other. However the history of philosophy instances theories which were consistent and at the same time in direct opposition to each other. Clearly they were not equally true; in fact the idealists themselves endeavor to disprove many of them. The same may be said of scientific hypotheses. We may have several rival internally consistent hypotheses striving for acceptance.

[11] Spaulding, *op. cit.*, p. 345.

The final decision as to the truth-claims of each is made not on the perfection of their consistency, but on their agreement with facts.[12]

The Pragmatic Theory of Truth

The essential doctrine of pragmatism is, as has been said, that we give assent to those beliefs which satisfy our needs and desires. The application of this doctrine to the problem of the nature of truth obviously necessitates a redefinition of truth. Truth cannot mean for the pragmatist what it means to the realist or the idealist. If we give credence to beliefs which are emotionally satisfying those beliefs are true which have satisfactory consequences, which work out in practice, which are useful in furthering our designs. We can only ascertain the working value of a belief through experience. The truth of a theory is not known immediately—it must be tested in the light of its results. Every belief has a truth-claim. If we find that the latter is warranted by the fruitful results consequent upon the working out of the belief in practice the belief becomes true; its claim to be true is validated. Our experience however is finite and hence no belief can be absolutely true. Furthermore, since it is the human mind which bends reality to serve its emotional satisfactions, it is the human mind which makes truth.

The extreme school of pragmatists goes further and affirms that not only is utility the sign of truth but that utility is truth. "The truth of an idea is not a stagnant property inherent in it. Truth *happens* to an idea. It *becomes* true, is *made* true by events. Its verity *is* in fact an event, a process; the process namely of its verifying itself, its veri-*fication*. Its validity is the process of its valid-*ation*."[13]

If James is to be taken literally our beliefs are not true

[12] See Walker, *op. cit.*, p. 506.
[13] James, *Pragmatism*, p. 201.

until they are verified, and their verification is their production of satisfactory results.[14]

The question of the validity of the pragmatic criterion of truth will be considered in the next chapter. Here we shall examine the answer of the more radical pragmatists to the question: what is the meaning of truth? Their answer is, utility. However the arguments adduced to establish this position, even if the truth of the pragmatic account of the nature of knowledge is granted, do not beget conviction.

The pragmatic dialectic is vitiated by the fallacy of equivocation; the term "meaning" is used in two senses. "Meaning" may signify (a) causal connection, or (b) symbolic connection. We may say, "Clouds mean rain," and *"Imber* means rain." In the second proposition, "mean" signifies that "imber" and "rain" are synonymous symbols for the same reality. In the first proposition "mean" signifies that clouds cause rain. It is evident that the two contents of the word "mean" are entirely different.

The pragmatist avers that we hold those beliefs are true which are satisfactory. He then goes on to say that the fact that a belief is satisfactory impels us to affirm that belief to be true. He makes the second deduction that satisfactoriness is therefore the meaning of truth. The equivocation is clear. When we ask the meaning of truth we do not use the term "meaning" in its causative sense. We are seeking the significance or content or "meaning" of the term "truth." We are not seeking the reasons or motives which beget truth in us. This definition of truth is therefore inept; it is not a definition of truth.[15]

---

[14] Many pragmatists do not attempt to sustain this radical position. See Murray, *Pragmatism,* pp. 45-46.
[15] For a further criticism of the pragmatic theory of truth consult MacIntosh, *The Problem of Knowledge,* p. 401; Pratt, *What Is Pragmatism?* lectures 2 and 3; Moore, *Philosophical Studies,* chap. 3; Walker, *op. cit.,* passim.

The Relativity of Truth. The relativity of truth is a doctrine peculiar to pragmatism. In the correspondence and coherence theories truth is absolute. This means that the nexus between the subject and the predicate of a true judgment is so firm and fixed that it is independent of persons, times, and places, i.e., it does not change with the different persons who make the judgment, or with the times and places in which the judgment is made. Once true is always true. Truth is said to be relative if it changes with the persons who are judging, or with the times and places in which a true judgment is made.[16]

Many pragmatists hold to the relativity of truth. They believe that truth is not absolute or fixed; on the contrary it is in a state of "making" or evolution. Once true is not always true. What is true for men in one age ceases to be true, and even becomes false, and is supplanted by a truth different from, or contradictory of and incompatible with, the former truth, when society has progressed to a new state of development. In time the supplanting truth will be in turn supplanted by a new truth, and the former will then be false.[17]

The doctrine of the relativity of truth is a direct consequence of the pragmatic theory of truth. It has achieved considerable vogue in our day and one reason for its popularity

---

[16] Relative in relation to knowledge has various meanings. It may signify: (1) agnostic relativism—the view that all we know in perception is the phenomenon. This is the position of positivism. (2) Kantian relativism, i.e., reality is so shaped by the mind in the knowledge process that we can never know it as it is; our knowledge is relative to the constitution of our minds. (3) Subjective relativism: nothing is true in itself—but only relatively to the individual; there is no objective truth. The classic expression of this theory is, "Man is the measure of all things"—an axiom subscribed to by Protagoras and Schiller. (4) Relativism in the sense explained above.

[17] Schiller, for example, speaks of errors as "discarded ex-truths"; they "were 'truth' in their day." *Studies,* pp. 212-213. Sidgwick says that "all truths are pro-tem truths at best, and the duration of their validity is uncertain." *Journal of Phil.,* Vol. II, 1905, p. 269.

is its apparent connection with the theory of evolution. The latter theory has centered attention on the extent of change in the universe. It is natural that the concept of change should be enlarged so as to include not only the realm of reality but the mental realm as well. But while the extension of the concept of change is natural it is not justifiable, as reflection will show. In the first place, change has no meaning unless the terms of the change-process remain unchanged. I cannot speak of a human being changing from an infant to a man, or of an acorn evolving into an oak, unless the terms "infant," "man," "acorn," and "oak" retain their significations unchanged. And what is true of terms is true of the judgments which are made up of terms. If the judgment, "The World War began in 1914" was true in 1914 (or in any other year), then it will always be true under penalty of losing its significance. The war might have ceased later but that fact would not alter the truth of the judgment. Physical processes may change but the judgments we make concerning them, if true, cannot change. Hence it would seem that the attempt to extend the notion of evolution from the physical field to the logical field is unwarranted.[18]

CRITICISM: Truth is relative in a certain sense.

(1) Human knowledge increases both in extent and content. But this growth does not imply that the true becomes the false or *vice versa*. The advance of knowledge involves the discarding of various hypotheses and theories in favor of new ones. But this only means one of two things. (a) If the older hypothesis is true the new hypothesis is but a fuller statement of facts—it is a more adequate explanation. (b) If the older hpothesis was thought to be true, but was in reality false as the new theory has proved, then it was false all the time; it never was true. For example, the geocentric theory was held quite universally for centuries. It was proven

[18] See Montague, *op. cit.*, p. 159; St. Thomas, *Summa*, I, 16, 9.

to be false and the heliocentric theory was substituted for it. But the true did not become the false; there was no evolution of truth into falsity because the geocentric theory never was true. The fact that hypotheses shift and change is an argument against the evolutionist theory of truth. Hypotheses are rejected when they are discovered to be untrue; they are never rejected when they are in agreement with facts.

(2) The same truth may influence different minds in different degrees. Similarly the influence of a truth may vary in different epochs or in different localities. This does not mean, however, that truth is relative in the evolutionary sense of the term; it does not mean that the doctrine is true for some and false for others, or true in some places and false in others. Neither does it imply that truth changes with time. It simply implies that the effects of truth vary—not truth itself.

(3) Again, it is obviously true that the judgment, "This is the fourth of July," which we will suppose is true, will be false if repeated to-morrow. But it is clear that to-morrow's judgment will not be false if we predicate "the fourth of July" of the same predicate, viz., yesterday. The judgment will then be, "This day (yesterday) was the fourth of July," and it will be true.[19]

Truth is absolute. Truth is not relative; the same judgment cannot be true for some and false for others, neither can it be true at one time and place and false in other times and places. Our reason for this belief is: truth is contained in a true judgment. A true judgment represents faithfully the real state of affairs; it is objective, it corresponds with the evidence of the reality of which it is made. But the real state of affairs, the object or reality of which the judgment is made, is one; it cannot be two or more contradictory states.

[19] See Coffey, *Logic,* Vol. I, p. 161.

Hence it cannot be truly represented in different minds by different judgments. The same argument holds good for the supposed variation of truth with time and place.[20]

The inconsistency of relativism. Another argument against this theory is based on its inconsistency. This theory is put forth as true. But if all truth changes, then the truth of the pragmatic theory changes. But this means that there will come a time when all truth will not change—as there may have been such a time in the past. We may rightly ask the pragmatist, "Is your theory one that is true only to-day, but which was not true in the past, and which will not be true in the future? Will the time come when truth will not be relative but absolute?" They maintain, of course, that their theory is absolutely true, that it was true in the past, and that it will be true in the future. But this is to say that the very theory which holds to the relativity of truth denies it. The inconsistency is patent.[21]

The Pragmatic and Coherence Theories Are Based on the Correspondence Theory

Both the pragmatic and coherence theories reject the correspondence theory. They both decry the doctrine that true knowledge corresponds to its object. They both set themselves up as being true theories, i.e., they both claim to give us the truth about the nature of truth. Pragmatism maintains that truth is utility; to a pragmatist that statement is indubitably true. Is truth what pragmatists say it is? If truth is what they say it is their theory corresponds to the reality about which it is made, viz., truth. The same may be said of the coherence theory. If the theory of coherence is true it represents truly the facts in question—it corresponds to the

---

[20] Coffey, *Epist.*, Vol. II, p. 232.
[21] Consult, Spaulding, *op. cit.*, p. 288.

facts. If neither of these theories corresponds to the facts they are false. The very statements of these theories, therefore, implies that their adherents implicitly admit the truth of the correspondence theory. The mere fact that pragmatists and idealists have elaborated theories of truth proves the truth of the correspondence theory.

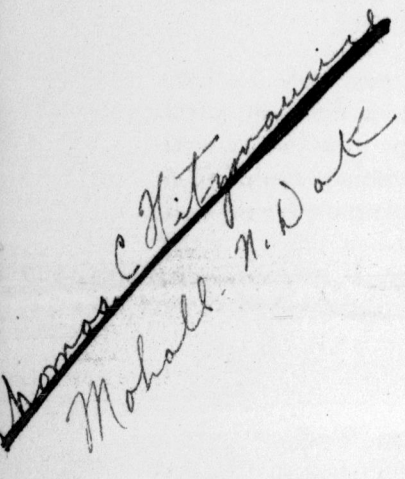

CHAPTER XVI

THE CRITERION OF TRUTH AND THE ULTIMATE MOTIVE OF CERTITUDE

THE criterion or test of truth is the standard which enables us to know our judgments are true. It is the norm which separates true from false judgments. By a motive of certitude is meant whatever moves or determines the mind to assent to a judgment as true. An ultimate motive of certitude is one that has no motive beyond it—no other to which we make a further appeal. We believe that the ultimate motive of certitude and the criterion of truth is one and the same—evidence.

Evidence

The Meaning of Evidence. The term "evidence" comes from the Latin *e-videre*—to see clearly. Etymologically, that quality of an object by which it is clearly visible is its evidence; that which the eye can see plainly is evident. Because of the analogy between the eye and the reason, the term was transferred from the object of ocular vision to the object of intellectual apprehension. Hence that which is objectively clear to the intellect is said to be evident, and that by which it is clear or evident is its evidence.

Kinds of Evidence. Existential evidence is the evidence we have for judgments of the real order, or for events, such as, "This is a book." Essential evidence (or evidence of possibility or impossibility) is evidence for judgments of the ideal order. This species of evidence prescinds from the actual existence of the objects represented by its concepts and is concerned with the essential relations between abstract aspects of reality. "The whole is greater than any of its parts," "No circle is a square," are examples for which we have essential evidence. When no reasoning is required to see the truth of a judgment, when, in other words, the judgment is self-evident, its evidence is said to be immediate. The evidence we have for the judgment. "This paper is white," is immediate. When the judgment is not self-evident, when reasoning is required to establish it, its evidence is mediate. We have mediate evidence for the judgment, "The sum of the angles of a triangle is equal to two right angles." When the evidence for a judgment is so cogent that it compels assent, it is said to be perfect, and when it does not compel assent, it is imperfect. Evidence is intrinsic when the reason for assent is in the reality about which the judgment is made, either mediately or immediately. When the reason for assent is the testimony of some authority, the evidence is extrinsic.

Evidence Is the Ultimate Motive of Certitude. Introspection shows us that the ultimate reason why we assent to a judgment with certitude is because the nexus between the subject and the predicate is clearly manifest to us. If we compare our certain assents with our states of doubt and opinion, we find that the reason we assent with certitude and do not remain in a state of doubt or assent provisionally is because the nexus is evident in the former case while it is not evident in the latter. We are certain because that which makes us assent—the nexus—is clear and obvious, or evident. This is true of judgments of the ideal order; it is also true of judgments of the real order. We have seen that we can have true knowledge of the physical order. And introspection tells us that when we form certain judgments about the extramental order we do so because we have evidence for them. For example, why do I say with certitude, "This is a book," or "This paper is white"? Because it *is* a book; because the paper *is* white. The objects of my judgments are clearly and evidently what I say they are, and because of this I cannot pronounce them to be otherwise. Evidence is then the ultimate motive of certitude; with it and because of it we are certain; without it there is and can be no certitude.

Evidence Is the Ultimate Criterion of Truth. Our judgments have to do with something distinct from the subjective act of judging. We make judgments about things and if they are to be true they must represent these things faithfully. If this be denied all our judgments are true simply because we make them. But we know that some of our judgments are false, and we know that they are false because the objects about which they are made are not as we judge them to be. Hence if we wish to know if a judgment is true or false it is clear that we must appeal to the evidence of the object about which the judgment is made. One can test his judgment by comparing it with its object, and in this way he can detect any difformity between the former and the latter.

This is the procedure in everyday life and it is also the criterion employed in the sciences. If we wish to verify our solution of a mathematical problem we go over the figures again to see if our second answer is the same as the first, i.e., we appeal to the evidence to see if the solution of the problem is really what we thought it to be. If we wish to verify our certitude that water is composed of hydrogen and oxygen we decompose water and see if these elements really combine to form water; we appeal to the evidence to see if water is really what we thought it to be. Evidence is the criterion of truth because evidence is the object as clearly known to us, and it is the only infallible and universal criterion by which we can test our knowledge.

This seems so obvious that the very simplicity of our solution may be disappointing. But we must not expect too much from a criterion of truth. We do not maintain that our criterion will do away with error. We simply affirm that evidence is the criterion of truth, and that it is not really distinct from the reality which reveals itself to the mind; neither is it distinct from the truth of which it is the criterion. The test of the truth of a judgment is ultimately the reality itself manifest to the mind. Our theory thus disposes of the difficulty urged by Montaigne.[1] Our criterion is intrinsic to the truth and is thus its own justification.

Many objections have been raised against this theory. The chief of these may be summarized as follows: it happens not infrequently that what appears to be evidence is not evidence at all. We know from experience that we have been deceived by appearances and illusions which won our assent because they seemed to be evident, whereas they were not. Hence it is said that evidence is useless and impractical as a test of truth since it must be itself tested.

We do not maintain that evidence is a magic charm, a touchstone, which will infallibly guarantee the truth of judgments. It is not a mechanical device which is applied to a judgment as a T-square is applied to a board. Neither is it something presented to us ready-made. Evidence does need testing in the sense that we must scrutinize what purports to be evidence with all the powers at our command before we accept it as evidence. We do not hold that we can, because of our criterion, exempt the mind from painstakingly examining the data presented to us. We only maintain that once we have the evidence we have an infallible criterion of truth, and that we can, if we observe due caution, obtain evidence for at least some of our judgments.

It has been said that our criterion is used in the physical sciences. May it not be held that the great achievements of the physical sciences is due, in part at least, to the fact that

[1] See above, p. 33.

scientists are scrupulous in their appeal to evidence as the test of truth? Are not these conquests to be explained by the readiness of scientists to cast aside as false whatever does not square with the facts? On the other hand, may we not explain the survival of many of the perennial disputes of philosophers by the refusal of the latter to abide by the decision of evidence? They, like other men, should listen to truth, they should not dictate to it; they should not attempt to make truth, they should discover it. They should remember that truth is not necessarily the intellectually palatable—that it is not necessarily that which satisfies the demands of a system. Philosophies, no matter how ingenious they may be, must be based on factual evidence or they are worthless.

Finally, we put this question to those who reject evidence as a test of truth: why do you hold to your own criterion of truth? Their reply is of course, that it is true—it is the true criterion. What is this but another way of saying that they have evidence for the truth of their own theory? It would seem that they implicitly admit evidence is the criterion of truth in their very attempt to deny it.[2]

Other Criteria of Truth

Many thinkers, because of the prevalence of error in human thought, reject evidence as the criterion of truth. Some of these seek refuge in skepticism, while others, believing that true knowledge is possible, find the criterion of truth in: (1) something extrinsic to the subject and object of knowledge, such as divine revelation, tradition, the common sense of mankind, etc., or (2) something intrinsic in the knowing subject, such as instinct, the will to believe, need, utility, etc. We believe that none of these positions is tenable. Once evidence is rejected there is no other criterion which can

---

[2] Consult Vance, *op. cit.*, p. 238; Coffey, *Epist.*, Vol. II, p. 245; Walker, *op. cit.*, p. 621; Jeannière, *op. cit.*, p. 244.

assure us of the truth of our convictions. We shall consider some of these attempts to substitute other criteria for evidence.

Fideism and Traditionalism. Fideism is the name given to the system of Huet (1630-1721), who taught that without the aid of divine revelation the human mind could never transcend mere probability; certitude is beyond its reach. Left to itself human reason is an unsafe guide to truth. An act of faith was necessary for the individual in search of truth. Traditionalism is the name given to that theory which maintains that the truths revealed to mankind by God and handed down (tradere—to deliver) in the tradition of the Catholic Church were the ultimate criterion of truth. Both these systems held that only those truths which squared with the teachings of the Catholic Church were true.[3]

CRITICISM: Before I can use the teachings of the Catholic Church as a criterion of truth I must be assured of (and therefore have evidence for) these facts: (1) that God exists; (2) that He has made a revelation; (3) that this revelation is embodied in the teachings of the Catholic Church. The ultimate criterion of truth is that which does not presuppose other tests by which it may be justified. It is clear that the teachings of the Catholic Church cannot be the ultimate criterion of truth. Again, if we test this theory by itself we find it is inconsistent, since we do not find it in the tradition of the Church. Nowhere does the tradition of the Church teach that it is the ultimate criterion of truth. Then too, it is manifestly impractical. A criterion of truth must be such that it can be applied to all truths of whatever kind. It is clear that the truths of revelation can serve as tests for but a few of the judgments we make.

---

[3] The most noteworthy of the traditionalists were De Bonald (1754-1840), De Lammenais (1782-1864), Bautain (1795-1867), Bonnetty (1798-1879), Ventura (1792-1861).

De Lammenais substitutes the dictates of the common sense of mankind for the dictates of the individual reason. The supreme criterion of truth for him is not the evidence given to the individual mind, but the agreement of all men is assenting to a judgment as true. If all men say a judgment is true, it is true; only those judgments are true which cohere with the universal beliefs of mankind. The errors of this view are easily seen.

(1) All men agree on a certain judgment because each individual assents, and each individual assents because he is convinced of its truth, which is another way of saying that he has evidence for it. Introspection shows us this. (2) How can an individual know: (a) that all men assent to a judgment; (b) that even if they do assent they may not all be mistaken, as has been the case; (c) that the common assent is a reliable test of truth? A rational being cannot employ this criterion until he can answer these questions affirmatively, and he can do this only if he has evidence for them. Hence this criterion is not ultimate.

The Pragmatic Criterion. The pragmatists hold that utility is the criterion of truth; that theory or belief is true which functions satisfactorily, which is effective in the production of results. The fact that a theory is useful is not proof positive that the theory is true. Utility points only to a presumptive belief in the truth of the theory. If a theory is not productive of results, if it is impractical, it is probably false. If a theory is useful we should be stimulated to an investigation of its truth-claim to see if it can be verified. This method of arguing for or against a system from its consequences is no modern innovation. It was used by the medieval scholastics.[4]

But they held, as we do, that it is only indirect and confirmatory. Our reasons for this position are: it is not incon-

[4] It was known to them as the *argumentum ex consectariis*.

ceivable that a movement which is fundamentally wrong may produce results which are suitable and which work in an eminent degree. For example, patriotism, a good thing in itself, has often been intensified by propaganda which was utterly false. It is not unthinkable that systems of thought which are wrong may issue in some good results—in the fields of religion and education, for example. Then again, two incompatible bodies of doctrine may work equally well. The criterion of usefulness would seem to be inept in this instance. Besides there are many judgments, whose truth we would like to know, such as those of higher mathematics, astronomy, history, etc., which have no bearing on either social welfare or individual happiness. How could we apply the test of utility to them?

Utility is based on evidence. Pragmatists hold that a theory is true if it is successful, if it is a belief enlarging human life. But what is the end or purpose of human life? Until I know the end to be attained, until I know the purpose of life, I cannot know whether the working out of my opinions will be good or bad, i.e., whether they are true or false. If the end is one thing my judgment might be good (or true) since it tends to that end; but if the end is something else, that same judgment is bad (or false) since it tends away from that end. Hence before I can know the suitability or utility of a judgment I must know the end to be attained. I can judge of the suitability of the means only in the light of my knowledge of the end. And I can only know the end when it is evident to me.

The truth of a judgment is not its utility, neither is the latter an ultimate criterion of truth, since, if it is to be of value, it must presuppose a knowledge of the true. A belief is useful because it is true; it is not true because it is useful. A judgment can work satisfactorily if it is true, if it agrees with facts, but its efficiency in producing results comes from its truth. If a judgment has satisfactory consequences it is probably true, but if it is true its truth was not determined by its satisfactory results, but by the fact that it agreed with the reality about which it was made.

Pragmatists seem to have overlooked this salient fact. They tell us that new theories are keys. If they open the doors of the unknown to us, i.e., if they issue in fruitful results, they are true. But they forget that while it is true a key is good because it opens a door, it opens the door not by chance, but because it conforms to the structure of the lock. Analogously, a theory will produce permanent beneficent results when it conforms with reality, when it is true.

If examined from a logical standpoint the inherent weakness of the pragmatic position is easily seen. From the evidently true proposition, "All true theories work," they infer the proposition, "All theories that work are true." This is an illicit inference as logic tells us. A universal affirmative proposition cannot be converted simply unless the subject and predicate have the same extension. But in the above proposition the fact that the extensions of the subject and the predicate coincide has not been, and cannot be, proved. One might make the logically correct inference, "No theories which do not work are true," but then he would have a negative criterion which would be of service only in the detection of error. The positive criterion of pragmatism cannot guarantee us the possession of truth.[5]

This criterion is inconsistent. On the supposition that the theory which works is true, our theory that the criterion of truth is evidence is true, since it works and is eminently satisfactory, at least for us. Why then do not the pragmatists

---

[5] See Hocking, *The Meaning of God in Human Experience*, Preface, p. 13.

accept it? They maintain that it is not true—that no non-pragmatic theory is true.⁶

Consistency demands that they should grant the same test to other theories that they claim for their own. The fact of the matter is that they cannot consistently hold that usefulness is either a mark of truth or that it is identical with truth.⁷

The pragmatic theory of truth seems indefensible. It involves such untenable tenets as these: (1) we can verify our true ideas; (2) only those ideas we can verify are true; (3) all our ideas are useful; (4) only those ideas which are useful are true; (5) we not only make our beliefs but we make them true.⁸

The Criteria of Sentiment, Instinct, Feeling. Many of the theories which reject evidence as the ultimate criterion of truth are anti-intellectualistic. They are so called because they hold that certitude is not based on an intellectual apprehension of reality but on a dictate of custom, sentiment, or feeling. In this class there are, first of all, the social pragmatists, who make the criterion of social and religious beliefs the social authority combined with individual religious instincts.⁹

We should hold to our religous and moral creeds not because we can justify them intellectually—this is impossible—but because custom prompts their acceptance. "Certitude is found to be the child, not of reason, but of custom." We should put our trust in our non-rational impulses and yearnings. Another group of thinkers rejects evidence and sets up as their criterion common sense—a blind instinct which

---

⁶ James, *Pragmatism*, lects. 3, 4; *A Pluralistic Universe*, lects. 1, 2, 3.
⁷ See Spaulding, *op. cit.*, p. 301.
⁸ See G. E. Moore, *op. cit.*, p. 100.
⁹ As typical advocates of this theory Balfour, Mallock and Brunetière may be cited.

is inherent in all of us and which is infallible.[10] The theory of sentimentalism, fostered by Jacobi (1743-1819), postulates the existence of a higher faculty, "reason," a spiritual sense, by whose dictates we believe in realities whose existence cannot be intellectually justified. This reason operates instinctively and is independent of the operation of our wills.[11]

Lastly, and widely held to-day, there is the moral dogmatism of Kant. He, as we have seen, held that the knowledge of the pure reason cannot transcend the phenomena. Hence the existence of God, the immortality of the soul, and the freedom of the will, cannot be proved by the speculative reason. Nevertheless these three realities exist and we believe in their existence, not because we can justify our belief intellectually, but because a dictate of our moral nature gives us a sufficient motive to believe in them.[12]

CRITICISM: In criticism of the above theories, and of all anti-intellectualistic theories, we submit the following argument: no feeling, or disposition, or inclination of man's nature can issue a dictate which can or ought to be accepted by man as the test of truth, constituted as he is with the power of reason. If we give credence to the dictate of a non-rational faculty we do so either blindly, or because we are convinced that the dictate is true. But why should we believe blindly in the dictate of any faculty? The existence of the faculty of reason cannot be gainsaid, and it forces me to ask the reason of my assents. In this instance it compels me to ask: Why should I believe in the dictate of a non-rational

[10] Thomas Reid (1710-1796) was the founder of this school. Among his followers may be mentioned Oswald, Beattie, and Stewart.
[11] Fries subscribes to a somewhat similar view as does Leonard Nelson.
[12] Among influential thinkers who follow Kant in this regard are Schleiermacher, Ritschl, and Sabatier.

faculty? It ill befits a rational creature to be irrational and hence if I cannot answer this question, if I do not know why the faculty should be believed, I should doubt its value and become a skeptic. If, on the other hand, I know why the faculty is to be believed, if I know that it is trustworthy, then its value is evident to my intellect, and the motive of my assent is ultimately intellectual. On this alternative anti-intellectualistic criteria rest ultimately on evidence.

Anti-intellectualism, in one form or another, has a large following among contemporary thinkers. But the substitutes offered to take the place of the intellect have their own disadvantages. Radical empiricism, mysticism, intuitionism, all have put forth their substitutes for the intellect. To the epistemologist no experience, whether it be pure, mystical, or intuitive, can serve as a source of philosophic truth until it has been scrutinized by the intellect. Every theory of knowledge must validate its sources of knowledge. It cannot, therefore, refuse to reflect upon its experiences, to analyze them, and to attempt to justify them. We cannot muzzle the intellect; it persists in asking, "Why?" Why must we accept the promptings of this or that feeling, this or that experience, this or that intuition? We have intellects and we cannot deny them a hearing. We do not maintain that the intellect is a perfect faculty of thought; we admit its limitations. But it seems more reasonable to use it in the light of its limitations than to discredit it absolutely. In other words, we cannot solve this problem, and the problem of knowledge in general, by making an intelligent being unintelligent.

The Will to Believe. Much is made to-day of the "will to believe" as a substitute for the intellect. Pragmatists have been ingenious in their efforts to identify the satisfaction of the reason with the satisfaction of the will. But the identification will not stand analysis. There is a clear-cut distinction between the satisfaction of the intellect and the satisfaction

of the will. When we strive to satisfy the will we are endeavoring to realize a good, and this means an effort on our part to conform our environment to our desires. When we are seeking the satisfaction of the intellect our procedure is the opposite. We then strive to make our judgments conform to reality—to make our minds reflect the nature of our environment. There is much in our environment that we cannot change to suit our desires, but we can know it as undesirable. There are things in nature which we can know truly, and we know they are not good, i.e., we know them but we do not desire them. And there are many things which we desire were true, but which we know are not true. Hence to insist on an identification of the satisfaction of our minds with the satisfaction of our wills is a glaring ineptitude. We must not attempt to gloss over the distinction between what we know to be true, and what we wish were true, between what is and what ought to be.

Concluding Remarks on the Criterion of Truth

We have asserted that objective evidence is the ultimate criterion of truth. We believe that reality presented to the mind is the ultimate court of appeal in the decision between the true and the false. But this does not mean that cogent evidence is the only kind of evidence, and that assent is to be confined to judgments for which we have such evidence. Most of our judgments are not irresistible. Our motives for adhering to them are not cogent although they may be sufficient. We recognize the existence and value of a number of secondary criteria. In practical life we cannot document every statement, analyze every theory, or inquire into the evidence of every fact, nor do we try to do so. We admit, for example, that the pragmatic criterion is useful, that it establishes a presumption in favor of the truth of a judgment. But we maintain that secondary criteria, while helpful, are but secondary, and that they but give us probability. The supreme, ultimate criterion must ever be evidence; it alone can give us certitude. We may appeal to as many secondary criteria as we like but in the end we must come back to evidence as the only criterion that can safeguard us against error.

While thus deferring to the demand of modern philosophers for a criterion of truth, it is well to note that what we really need is a criterion of error. Once grant, as all but skeptics do, that valid knowledge is possible, it follows that our minds must, if properly used, give us the truth, since it is absurd to suppose that our minds do not know what they know. What we need are not criteria which tell us when we have gone right, but criteria which tell us when we have gone wrong, viz., which will aid us in detecting any influence, subjective or objective, which may have wrongfully determined the content of our thought.

CHAPTER XVII

THE TRUTH OF KNOWLEDGE

We can now answer the second question proposed at the beginning of this discussion: Is knowledge valid? Is the validity of knowledge a philosophically established certitude? In the light of what has been said the question can be unhesitatingly answered in the affirmative: Knowledge is valid.

The Truth of Perceptual Knowledge

Our percepts, when formed in accordance with and under the influence of the evidence of the objective world, when conditioned by the objects they represent, are true. Introspection reveals the fact that we can and do form our percepts under the influence of the extramental world—it shows us that our percepts are objective. Hence they are valid representations of reality.

The Truth of Concepts

We have established the fact that we have concepts.[1]

The truth-value of concepts has been disputed by those who profess the theory of conceptualism. This theory admits the existence of abstract, universal concepts, but it denies that they have a basis in extramental reality; they have an ideal value only. They cannot be proved to have a real value, i.e., they cannot be proved to give us a valid insight into the nature of reality revealed to us by the senses. Con-

[1] See above, p. 57.

ceptualism does not enjoy the popularity of nominalism—its adherents being limited to practically two schools of thought, the Kantian and the pragmatic.

Conceptualism is given a certain amount of plausibility by the fact that while we cannot doubt the existence of universal concepts their relation to sense data is not easily seen. Sense data are so real as compared with the abstract tenuous character of concepts that the reality and worth of the latter are apt to be suspected. Reflection will remove this prejudice against the objectivity of concepts and it will show us that it is but a prejudice which would force us to the odd conclusion that while the senses may make us aware of reality the intellect cannot know it.

Kantian Conceptualism. We have seen that Kant held that the mind can apprehend only the product of the synthesis of the categories of the understanding and the manifold given in sense intuition, viz., the phenomenon. The very constitution of the mind forbids our knowing the noumenon. Through the operations of the categories concepts are formed but they have only a phenomenal value. They can give us no knowledge of the nature of reality. They have no contact with reality as unaffected by the categories, and hence we have no warrant for establishing a correspondence between our concepts and reality. Kantian conceptualism is an integral part of his system as a whole and hence it needs no refutation. His conceptualism is necessitated by the dialectic of the rest of his theory of knowledge and it stands or falls with that system. However a direct examination discloses evident defects, of which but two shall be mentioned.

Consistency demands that Kant should have only one category instead of twelve. In his theory the categories combine or synthesize systematically the manifold of sense intuition. The latter is a chaotic manifold of isolated sense impressions which are unknowable in themselves. When the latter stimulate the categories into activity it seems that they should rouse into activity one and the same category. An unknown chaotic manifold cannot call into activity different categories, since in itself it is undifferentiated. Even if a plurality of categories be granted the difficulty still remains of explaining how one category should be called into operation rather than another. Kant is unable to show how the same sensible impression sets into operation now this, now that category.[2]

Kant holds that conception is a process whereby the mind makes or constructs its thought-objects. Thought is manufacture.[3]

But this contradicts the very nature of knowledge. There is a fundamental difference between making and knowing. Knowledge presupposes that the thing known already exists, else it could not be known. Knowing is an awareness of that which is. Even if the reality known is something we make, our knowledge of it is clearly distinct from our creation of it. Introspection informs us that we do not construct or manufacture the objects of our knowledge, but that our knowledge of those objects is subsequent to, and dependent on their existence.

Pragmatic Conceptualism. The pragmatist attack on the worth of concepts is in line with the general attitude of pragmatism as regards the function of knowledge. Knowledge is practical, and concepts are merely instrumental, "tools slowly fashioned by the practical intelligence for the mastery of its experience."[4]

Concepts are "tallies" by which we tabulate our impressions.[5]

They are, to use James' figure, like the seven-league boots of the fairy tale; they enable us to travel with speed and

---
[2] See Mercier, *Crit. Gen.*, p. 383; Prichard, *op. cit.*, p. 214.
[3] Prichard, *op. cit.*, pp. 211-212; p. 234.
[4] Schiller, *Studies in Humanism*, p. 64.
[5] James, *Pragmatism*, p. 171.

expedition over the entire realm of our experiences. They thus have a purpose and they serve a useful end. They assist materially in the orderly arranging of our knowledge. Because we can form universals we are freed from the bondage of the here and now, and we can rise to the plane of generality. But the virtues of the concept are offset by its defects. It is a mental construct and hence it is not a true representation of the reality we sense. Its misrepresentation of reality arises from its abstractness. Being abstract it does not represent reality in all its richness. Yet intellectualistic thinkers use concepts as if they stood for the whole object.[6]

The pragmatists are correct in their affirmation that concepts are tools; it is through the use of concepts that we think, form systems of thought, and fabricate philosophies of life. But are concepts only tools? Do they not reveal reality to us? Are they not means whereby we interpret reality? If they are means of knowledge, a point we shall attempt to prove, and if their primary function is to enable us to understand what we experience, then it is apparent that the reason they are tools which aid us in the manipulation of what we experience is because they reveal reality to us. The pragmatists with their usual emphasis on the practical aspect of knowledge have overlooked the fact that the essential note of knowledge is its content.

As to James' view that the abstract character of concept results in a "vicious intellectualism" which misrepresents reality, we reply that this is not the fault of the concepts. Vicious intellectualism arises from the misuse of concepts. There is a class of minds which is prone to make abstractions real, which does not distinguish between abstract aspects of reality

[6] Bergson goes still further in his disparagement of the concept. He claims that it is not only misused but that it positively falsifies the presentment of reality. See *Creative Evolution*, Eng. trans., p. 46.

and reality itself. But this does not disprove the value of concepts as modes of thought when rightly used. One might similarly argue that the fact of error proves that knowledge is worthless. The attacks of the more radical thinkers, such as Bergson, who claim that conceptual knowledge distorts reality, are due to the exigencies of their systems. They are anti-intellectualists and as such they disparage the worth of all intellectual knowledge; the concept falls quite naturally under their censure. But, as has been indicated above, when an anti-intellectualist argues against the worth of the intellect he places himself in the embarrassing position of using the intellect to forge arguments which deny the validity of the very means whereby they have been established. His arguments nullify themselves.

The Relation of the Individual to the Universal. The validity of concepts has been attacked from another angle. The fact that concepts are abstract while the existent realities of which they are sometimes predicated are concrete is made the basis of another objection. It is alleged that the assigning of different attributes to the object in nature and to the same thing as conceived vitiates the value of the concept. This procedure creates an antinomy between the world of reality and that same world as represented in thought. We cannot, therefore, predicate a universal concept of a singular concrete thing. We cannot formulate a judgment such as, "This is a man," because in so doing we are identifying an abstract concept "man" with a singular concrete "this."

This objection overlooks the fact that it is the content (or meaning) of the concepts that we predicate and not their universality or abstractness. The content of the concept is really in the individual realizations of which it is predicated, and hence it can be rightly predicated of them. We know that it is in them because it was abstracted from them. Abstraction is not falsification. It is simply the intellectual representation of the nature or essence of the reality. It is true that we experience only particular objects, but each of these has a nature which belongs to it just as much as does its position in time and space. Abstraction is not the fabrication or creation of something different from what is experienced—it is merely the presentation to the intellect of the nature of the object. When the abstractive process is rightly carried out the representation is faithful and the concept is true.

But while the representation is faithful it is not adequate. It gives us nothing of the individuating notes found in all individuals besides their nature. Each individual thing is more than the concept represents it to be. But the concept, while inadequate, is true as far as it goes, for it reveals what is truly in the individual. For example, the nature of man is really in James and John because the concept "man" represents the nature of each. They both have those essential notes which go to constitute manhood. Therefore it is legitimate for us to predicate "man" of both of them; we can rightfully enunciate the judgments, "James is a man," and "John is a man." It is true that both of them are more than mere men; they both have their own qualities which differentiate them from all other men. These latter qualities are not represented in the concept "man." But while both of these individuals have much that is not in the concept "man" there is nothing in that concept which is not in them, and hence it is a valid, if inadequate, representation of them.

Again, the universalizing of the concept adds nothing to its content. It is merely a mental addition which, while it enlarges the extension of the concept, does not alter its comprehension. The concept "man" whether it is a direct or reflex universal has the same content. The process of universalizing, therefore, does not affect the validity of the concept.

Proof of the Validity of Concepts. The proof of the validity of concepts is an easy step from the fact established above, viz., that we derive our concepts from sense knowledge.[7]

It may be summarized thus: the objects of intellectual concepts are contained in, and are derived from, the objects of sense knowledge. But the objects of sense knowledge are real. Therefore the objects of our concepts are real.

Introspection tells me that, in any individual thing I sense, I perceive not only the sense qualities, but that I also conceive notes which correspond to my ideas of "being," "substance," "life," etc. This indicates that the material object of my thought and of my senses is the same, i.e., that the object of my concept is really in, and materially identical with, the object of sense. So intimately are the processes of sensation and intellection intermingled that ordinarily I do not think of separating or distinguishing them. Spontaneously, I am apt to confound the object of my concept with the object of my percept, so that I have to make a deliberate effort to realize that there are taking place within me simultaneously two cognitive acts (conception and perception) which have a common material object.[8]

This is apparent in judgments whose predicates are concepts interpreting sense data, such as, "I see a man." In point of fact I see something colored, whereas I think or conceive the nature "man." The latter is only an object of vision accidentally, i.e., owing to the fact that what I see is, I know, a quality or an attribute of a man. Despite this fact we make judgments like the above, and our identifying of the conceptual predicate with the perceptual subject proves

[7] See above, p. 86.
[8] See Mercier, *Crit. Gen.*, p. 337.

that they—the subject and the predicate—have the same object.[9]

Another argument in favor of the view that conception and perception terminate in the same reality is that based on the dependence of our concepts on sense data. The fact of dependence cannot be gainsaid. (1) Abnormal conditions of the sensory apparatus lead to a disturbance and confusion of concepts. (2) Persons deprived of the use of a particular sense from birth do not have concepts which correspond to the data ordinarily furnished by that sense. (3) Communication of concepts is best accomplished by the arousing of percepts and images. The imparting of abstract ideas is facilitated by the use of images, symbols and the like. (4) Intellectual cognition is usually, if not always, accompanied by the activity of the senses and the imagination. These facts prove that there is an intimate dependence of concepts on percepts.

The Truth of Judgments

If our percepts and concepts are valid it follows that our judgments may also be valid. As regards judgments of the ideal order we have shown above that in enunciating them the intellect should be determined by the objective evidence, and that when so determined the judgments conform to reality, and hence are true. In enunciating judgments of the real order the intellect may also function validly. Our percepts are true representations of reality and when the intellect forms judgments under the guidance of reality as evidenced in the percepts its judgments are true.

---

[9] Introspection tells us therefore, "that the intellect finds in the data of sense experience its proper object, viz., the essence of things; it reads or deciphers in the core of the sense fact, 'that which the thing is,' to use an expression (*quidditas, quod quid est*) of St. Thomas who derives from the power of reading into (*intus legere*) the etymology of the word 'intellect.'" Mercier, *ibidem*, p. 380.

Reflection proves that when I make a judgment I conform my mind to the evidence; I attribute the predicate to the subject (or deny it of the subject) according as the predicate shows itself to be conjoined to the subject or not. If the evidence upon which the judgment is based is objective, it follows that the judgment is true. In other words, I affirm that "that is which is, and that that is not which is not," which is truth. Why do I know that my judgments conform to reality? *Because I make them in conformity with reality.*

The Validity of Deductive Reasoning. Deduction is that form of inference by which we advance from truths already known to other truths implied in the former. The typical expression of deduction is the syllogism. This starts from a universal premise and arrives at the truth of a conclusion which is implied in the truth of the premises. An example of a typical deductive syllogism is:

> All men are mortal.
> John is a man.
> Therefore John is mortal.

The syllogism has often incurred the censure of philosophers. As early as 200 A.D., it was attacked by Sextus Empiricus. Positivists, and anti-intellectualists have adopted a contemptuous attitude toward it. The discrediting of syllogistic reasoning is due partly to a misunderstanding of its value, and partly to a faulty theory of conception.

Mill has succinctly stated the popular objection to the worth of the syllogism.[10]

He says that we can never attain a knowledge of a universal proposition without having previously examined all the individuals under the extension of the universal. We cannot establish the truth of the universal premise until we know the truth of the conclusion. Thus in the syllogism:

[10] *Logic,* b. 2, chap. 3.

> All men are mortal.
> Socrates is a man.
> Therefore Socrates is mortal.

we cannot say, "All men are mortal" until we know the conclusion, viz., that Socrates is mortal, for if Socrates is not mortal then all men are not mortal. But if we know the truth of the conclusion before we begin to reason our reasoning is futile. On the other hand, if we assume the truth of the conclusion, we are assuming what we have to prove. If the conclusion is a new truth, i.e., one not contained in the premises, it does not follow from the premises, and if it does follow from the premises it is not new.

CRITICISM: We must distinguish between real syllogisms, i.e., syllogisms at least one of whose premises is a truly universal proposition, and apparent syllogisms. By the latter is meant syllogisms whose "universal" proposition is a collective or enumerative universal, viz., a proposition whose universality is attained by an enumeration of all the individuals in its extension. An example of such a syllogism is:

> All the Apostles were Jews.
> Peter was an Apostle.
> Therefore Peter was a Jew.

It is evident that I could not know the truth of the universal premise of this "syllogism" unless I had previously ascertained the truth of the conclusion. But such a congeries of propositions, while resembling a syllogism, is in reality not a syllogism. It is not even a process of inference since the conclusion does not increase our knowledge. Mill is justified in his charge that such apparent syllogisms are vitiated by the fallacy of begging the question.

But there are syllogisms whose universal premise is not enumerative but universal in the strict sense of the term.

Mill, because of his nominalism, denies that universal concepts can be formed, but in this he is wrong. And if universal concepts can be formed, propositions which are truly universal can be enunciated. That is to say, propositions whose universality has its basis and justification not in a complete enumeration of instances but in an analysis of the nature and attributes of the subject which they represent in thought. The true universal judgment is an enunciation of an abstract truth which is seen to apply necessarily and which applies, therefore, to all actual and possible instances under the universal.

The application of this statement to Mill's own example will clarify this point. I can be certain of the truth of the universal premise without being explicitly aware of the truth of the conclusion. The judgment, "All men are mortal," is but the universalized expression of the judgment, "Man as such is mortal," and this latter is an abstract judgment. It expresses a necessary truth, viz., the nature of man is a compound and is therefore subject to dissolution, or, in other words, is mortal. I arrive at the knowledge of this abstract truth not by an examination of every man, but by an analysis of the nature of man. And to analyze the nature of man only one man, or at most only a few men, need be examined, since all men have the same nature. An examination of all of them would be superfluous. Once the abstract truth is attained, it is universalized. It is in this way that we obtain universal judgments, or the major premises of true syllogisms, and it is apparent that we do so without previously knowing the truth of the conclusion.

This answer to the positivist attack on the worth of the deductive syllogism reveals to us the true worth of the syllogism. Deductive reasoning does not add to truth; it simply adds to our knowledge of the truth. Deduction makes actual and explicit knowledge that is only implicit and virtual. The premises contain the conclusion. If they did not we could not deduce it from them. Yet the truth of the conclusion cannot be actually known in the premises, else the reasoning would be superfluous. Hence it is in the premises latently and virtually; inference actualizes and explicitates it.

CHAPTER XVIII

THE CAUSES OF ERROR

The fact of error must be explained by any system of knowledge which claims that the mind is capable of achieving the truth. Especially is this true of the system we have set forth. For we have maintained that both the senses and the intellect are trustworthy, that they are both sources of true knowledge. If this theory is true it must be able to explain the fact of error—it must show that the existence of error is not incompatible with the validity of sensory and intellectual knowledge.

The mind can attain the truth but it is not forced or necessitated to attain the truth. If the latter were the case the origin of error would be inexplicable. As we have seen, knowledge is true when it represents reality faithfully. When the mind is guided in its pronouncements by the objective evidence of the reality about which the pronouncements are made, when there is a harmony between these pronouncements and the objective evidence, then the mind is in possession of truth. But when the mental representation is not a faithful representation of the object, when there is a difference between the objective evidence and the judgment made about it, the mind is in error.[1]

The search for the causes of error will resolve itself into

---

[1] Error may be defined as a positive difformity between the mind judging, or the mind's judgment, and the reality about which the judgment is made.

an attempt to enumerate the reasons why our judgments do not represent reality faithfully, or why there is a discord between our judgments and reality.

First of all, we must recall something said above, viz., that knowledge is not a mere passive awareness impressed on the mind by reality. Neither is it a passive mirroring of reality. The mind is not passive in the formation of knowledge—it is exceedingly active. We have knowledge only when we interpret reality, when we make judgments about it. And judgments are products of the mind's activity. A judgment is an active process of analysis and synthesis; it is a mental representation of reality accomplished by means of a mental affirmation or denial of a predicate of a subject. This activity on the part of the mind in the formation of judgments is the ultimate reason why reality is sometimes misrepresented and distorted in our judgments. The activity of the mind is not of itself the cause of error because the mind can and does attain the truth despite its activity. But the activity permits the operation of certain factors which influence the process of knowledge formation and it is these factors which are more properly the causes of error.

Introspection shows us that when the evidence for a judgment is cogent and compelling, as in the case of first principles, error seldom occurs. In these instances the evidence is so strong that the mind is forced to form judgments which correspond with reality. But in cases where the evidence is not cogent error is found not infrequently.

Objective Causes

Since knowledge has two aspects, the objective and the subjective, both these aspects must be taken into account in detailing the causes of error. Strictly speaking, the object of knowledge cannot be a cause of error. It can only move the mind to assent by reason of the evidence it presents, and hence it cannot determine the mind to make a false judgment. If the mind always made its judgments in accord with the evidence of the object there would be no error. The object may, however, be the occasion of error, in as much as its evidence may be so slight that the mind is led to make a false judgment concerning it. Or it may happen that the evidence is presented under abnormal circumstances, and the mind pronounces upon it without adverting to the abnormality. In both these instances the cause of the error is mental since the object is merely the occasion of the error.

Subjective Causes

The subjective causes of error are those which are in the subject and which tend to make the subject enunciate judgments which are at variance with the evidence. These causes are largely non-rational, i.e., they do not of themselves form part of the knowledge apparatus. The mind itself is not radically defective. But it is only one of the factors operating in the enunciation of judgments. Man is more than mind—he has non-rational faculties as well, and it is the functioning of these latter which interfere with the thinking process, and which are responsible in a great degree for the errors of thought. It is they which color and distort the evidence, which hurry the mind to a conclusion, which impel it to utter judgments which are not conditioned by the evidence. We shall enumerate some of the more important of these factors which make for error.

Aversion to Doubt. The undisciplined mind is averse to suspense and hesitation. An unsettled state of mind is not pleasant; it is irksome. Most men have not learned that certitude can be the result of objective evidence alone, and that when this is lacking judgment should be suspended. Being constitutionally impatient they hurry to a decision without examining what purports to be evidence, or even without requiring evidence. They have a predilection for premature acceptance of beliefs and a proneness for decision. They feel that they must have opinions on a great many questions and they are not happy until they adopt them. They do not base their judgments on reasoned grounds, although they persuade themselves that they do, and hence the opinion they adopt may or may not be true. It is not necessarily wrong but its truth or falsity is largely accidental. The fact of the matter is that a pressing need for a belief of some kind will not permit them to scrutinize and test the seeming evidence. Any tenet which offers a relief from doubt, any conviction that frees the mind from the irritant of hesitation is eagerly embraced.

It goes without saying that the mark of a critical mind is delay and suspense, pending inquiry and investigation. This is the essence of critical thinking. Assent should be measured by the strength of the grounds for assent. If the grounds warrant only provisional assent that assent should be given. Certain assent should be given only when the evidence deserves it. If we attempt to show how it is that we are so prone to be convinced by insufficient evidence we shall have to mention many influences operating on the mind, chief among which are the following.

Mental sloth. Mental sloth is a prevalent factor in the genesis of error. Men want to be certain but they do not want to go through the laborious steps which must preface the attainment of certitude. Truth must be sought after, and it can be achieved, especially if it be a truth worth while, only by cautious, painstaking, and persevering application. Men are averse to this because mental labor is often more tedious and difficult than manual labor. The tendency to minimum effort is as common in the realm of the mind as it is in the realm of nature. Hence they shirk the necessary steps that lead to certitude and in their haste to be certain they do not arrive at a certitude that is objective and true.[2]

School-thinking. Another widespread device which is embraced as a short cut to certitude is school-thinking. Men are social animals even in the domain of thought; they like to think gregariously. The fact that others think as we do gives us confidence in our own views. Hence our views are so often the views of our set. We become familiar with certain beliefs through frequently hearing them, and they become true for us by our long association with them. We forget that the opinions of others differ from our own; we stifle misgivings, we close our eyes to the evidence adduced by other schools of thought, and we thus become victims of self-opinionated error which is worse than ignorance. Familiarity can never serve as a measuring rod for truth. The school-thinker does not think; he remembers, he repeats, he is a routinist. Truth for him is what squares with the views of his associates. He seeks to maintain a view rather than to ascertain the truth. He lacks the essential note of a thinker—love of truth for truth's sake.[3]

The worth of authority. Most of our convictions are not the result of personal reflection and investigation. We are forced to depend upon the word of others for most of our convictions. The field of knowledge is so vast that it is morally impossible for one to authenticate his every view. Personal experience is so limited that it would give us but little knowledge were it not possible to join to it the experience of others, past and present. A little thought will show us that the current ideas of our age and our country, the phases of public opinion, the theory of the hour, are influences which constitute an intellectual atmosphere, and which go far in molding and coloring our beliefs. But it must be

[2] St. Thomas, *Summa*, 2, 2, q. 53, art. 2.
[3] St. Thomas, *II Meta.*, lect. 5.

remembered that the authority of human testimony is not an ultimate criterion of truth.

No man's authority is of value unless (1) he knows the truth, and (2) unless he is veracious. Unless we know that our authority is not deceived and that he is not deceiving us, it is perilous to assent to his views with certitude. It is manifestly quite difficult to establish the first of these conditions. Hence it is that arguments based on authority are the weakest of all arguments. A casual acquaintance with the history of philosophy, or with the history of any of the sciences, suffice to show that many of the so-called authorities are not authorities at all. The amount of error due to this sheep-like tendency of the human mind is appalling. To many minds the printed word is a sufficient motive of truth. They give unquestioning adherence to any doctrine provided it is found in a book. The shibboleths of the day are a sufficient guarantee of the truth to others. Many follow blindly the *ipse dixit* of the leader of their school. A mind of a critical temper will be chary of giving certain assents to view based on authority alone, unless it is assured that the authority is reliable. Recognizing the fallibility of the human mind, and the consequent fallibility of human authority, it will satisfy itself as to the worth of its authority before it gives it credence.

Self Interest. One of the most prevalent causes of error is the fact that we cannot view things in a detached, objective way. We cannot see them as they are. We view them through the distorting medium of our own desires, needs, and preferences. We see the world through the windows of the senses that are smeared with self-interest. Rarely do we look at it through disinterested eyes. Things are held to be true which we want to be true. We give certain assent to theories and doctrines which we cherish, which are pleasant, which do not jar our mental calm. It is a very common human trait to defend an opinion which results in personal gain. Only a hard-minded man can assent to facts which are distasteful and humiliating, or which issue in a loss of prestige or reputation. But it is obvious that likes or dislikes cannot serve as a criterion of truth. It is equally obvious that if one is to attain truth he must distrust his emotional and volitional impulses which prompt him to accept a doctrine, because they only too often color the doctrine and move the mind to embrace the false. The discriminating mind in sifting and scrutinizing the incoming impressions never asks, "What use is this to me?" but, "Is it true?" It views things as they are, and not in relation to itself. It is willing and anxious to attain the truth even though it be unpleasant. It has a horror of fact-shaping, i.e., of fitting facts to preconceived theories. It knows that sometimes the truth is drab and uninteresting in comparison with highly tinted error, and hence it scorns the spirit of dilettantism which prefers smartness or seeming brilliance to truth. It will not aim at being original or novel, but it will strive ever and always to find the truth, though its effort entail sacrifice and weariness and disappointment.

Efficient thinking requires that our views be kept free from emotional obscurity. We cannot think without mental complexes—without erecting systems of thought. But we should not forget that most of our complexes are formed under the influence of non-rational motives. Our thoughts must be kept free from all entangling alliances with self-interest and desire; they must be based on the objective states of affairs and on nothing else. He who does not recognize this fact and apply it rigorously is hopeless as a thinker.

Prejudice. Judgments formed under the preceding subjective conditions result in our becoming prejudiced. Oblivious of the fact which is evidenced by introspection, that most of our views are not objective but are flimsily founded, we persuade ourselves that they are the result of solid reasoning. Prejudices have gripped us unawares; we serenely fancy that we think out questions and settle them by reason alone. As a matter of fact we do not reason *to* most of our convictions at all; we reason *for* them. We crave consistency in our beliefs and hence the usual procedure is first to adopt a belief and then to find "reasons" for it. It is only after it has been attacked or questioned that we search for reasons to substantiate it. And then we defend it not because it is true but because it is ours. Self-love and an unwillingness to discard a cherished belief prompt us to spring to its defense.

The mental bias resulting from prejudice is destructive of clear thinking since it prevents our weighing impartially any evidence that contravenes our view. Because of our prejudices we "prejudge" the worth of a view which differs from our own; we do not examine it on its own merits but rather on the basis of its relation to our own view. It is wrong because it differs from our own theory, but if it happens to be in accord with our own theory it is true. Evidence means little to a prejudiced mind. It is very human to estimate the truth of new or contrary opinions in the light of the system that we have adopted. Especially is this true when the mind is confronted with facts which are dyed with self-interest. In this event the mind is like a faulty mirror—it distorts what it reflects. The evidence for the new facts is distorted, and they are thus easily gestured away. Not only do we minimize the evidence for unliked facts but we are often unable to understand the arguments of our opponents. We cannot follow lines of thought which antagonize a strong emotional prejudice. No adage is more trite than, "There are two sides to every question," yet to the uncritical mind there is usually only one side—its own. This dogged determination to cling to one's views often persists after one has feigned open-mindedness in considering opposing arguments. It nullifies a great deal of what passes for "thought" and it results in but a rearrangement of prejudices.

We prescind here from mentioning the fallacies of logic as causes of error, not because they are unimportant, but because their treatment belongs to that science. We omit also mention of the fallacies which are peculiar to the various fields of knowledge. Each field of knowledge has its own canons of thought which must be observed if the conclusions of that field are to be correct. Thus the inductive reasonings of scientists are often vitiated by fallacies which are proper to science. Among these are non-observation, mal-observation, false analogy, illicit generalization and the like.[4] Back of all the causes of error is the simple fact that we do not attain the truth because we do not love it, and not loving it sufficiently we are unwilling to make the sacrifices which the attainment of truth demands. The seeker after truth must know that the basic and fundamental quality which must distinguish him is a pure and disinterested love of truth. If this is lacking his effort to attain truth will be largely in vain. This love of truth must be deep-rooted and sincere for only then will it inspirit him to surmount the malignant influences of self-interest and desire, of partisanship and passivity, of sloth and superficiality, all of which tend to make him swerve from the path of his endeavor. He must learn that the "mind is below truth, not above it, and is bound not to descant upon it, but to venerate it."[5]

The pursuit of truth must be to him a sacred duty, and therefore one to which he will give the best efforts of his mind. He will be open-minded and fair; he will give an

[4] The classical causes of error are the "idols" of Francis Bacon. Another and older list is that of Roger Bacon as given in this Opus Majus.

[5] Newman, *Letter to the Duke of Norfolk*, 6.

impartial ear to those with whom he disagrees. Yet he will not permit his impartiality to degenerate into indifference, for his love of truth is a hatred of error. His way may be long and weary, it may turn a while from its goal, but he will pursue its windings with confidence for he knows that it is the only way which leads to that which alone can satisfy his mind.[6]

[6] See Wallas, *The Art of Thought;* Clarke, *The Art of Straight Thinking.* Burtt, *Principles and Problems of Right Thinking,* p. 3.

CHAPTER XIX

CONCLUSION

The aim of this elementary treatise is the investigation of the truth-claim of knowledge. In the prosecution of this aim the following problems were discussed: Does reflection justify certitude? Can the human mind attain certain knowledge? Skepticism, whose answer to both these questions is negative, was subjected to a critical examination; it was found to be unsatisfactory in view of the fact that it had failed to establish its contention. Dogmatism, which holds that man can achieve certain knowledge, was proposed as the true theory.

The question of the origin of our knowledge was then taken up. A priorism, intuitionism, pragmatism, sensism, pure rationalism, and critical rationalism all failed to satisfy the demands of thought. Moderate realism, a combination of empiricism and rationalism, was found to be the only system that accounted satisfactorily for the origin of our knowledge.

The question of the truth of knowledge revolved around the claims of realism and idealism, subjective and objective. The realistic standpoint was adopted, both as regards the independence of reality in relation to mind, and as regards the validity of our knowledge of the physical world. The existence of an extramental world was maintained against the claims of idealism. Our knowledge of the world was shown to be possible and true.

The nature of truth was subjected to scrutiny. The correspondence theory, despite its difficulties, was seen to be superior to both the coherence and the pragmatic theories.

The criterion of truth then engaged our attention. The criterion of evidence seemed to be preferable to the other criteria proposed. On the basis of this criterion the truth of perception, conception, judgment, and reasoning was established. Error was shown to be possible. While the mind is a source of true knowledge it is not necessitated to attain the truth.

The theory of knowledge which has been outlined in the preceding pages is in sharp opposition to two tendencies of modern thought. It disagrees in root and branch with any theory of an idealistic trend, which would hold that the representative aspect of knowledge is due to the mind's inner activity. It maintains that knowledge is, and must be, conditioned by the objective. It is also committed to the view that while knowledge is sensistic in origin it does not retain this sensory quality. There is a sharp cleavage differentiating it from all sensistic and positivistic theories.

Despite the fact that it stands aloof from various prevailing tendencies of thought, it is withal a philosophy of moderation. It pursues the difficult *via media* between the extremes which other systems of thought have embraced. To the idealist it seems pedestrian, and to the ultra-realist it seems at too far a remove from reality. Yet this is its very strength—that it occupies the median position between these two views. It offends the sensist by stressing the suprasensuous note in knowledge, while the intellectualist finds fault with its sensism. But here again perhaps its truth derives from the fact that it has escaped the extreme tendencies of both sensism and ultra-intellectualism.

Its position of detachment has made it a mark for a crossfire of criticism from other schools of thought. But this position is a position of advantage as well as of disadvantage, for it enables us to buttress our position by arguments drawn from other schools of thought. We utilize the destructive criticism of idealism on the part of the realists, and we profit by the strictures of idealism against ultra-realism. The ultra-intellectualist inveighs against the sensist, and the sensist points out the fallacy of ultra-intellectualism, while we build up an apologetic for our own tenets out of this mutual criticism.

The version of realism which has been expounded is a sober theory of knowledge. It is not lyric or impressionistic in its treatment of knowledge. It neither blinks the facts nor does it idealize them. Reduced to its simplest terms it maintains, (1) that there are minds and reality, and (2) that minds can know reality. Reality is more or less shrouded in darkness but the mind can know it notwithstanding. The mind has its limitations but it performs its functions reasonably well, and it can, as this treatise has endeavored to show, vindicate its claims to be a valid means to the achievement of truth.

INDEX

Abnormal sense perception, 140ff.
Absolute, the, 111, 119ff.
Abstraction, theory of, 89
Adams, 122
Adamson, 112
Aenesidemus, 5, 30
Agnosticism, metaphysical, 135
Albee, 113
Alexander, 100
Allen, 53
Anti-intellectualism, its teaching on concepts, 199; the criterion of truth of, 190ff.
Arcesilaus, 30
Ardigo, 53
Aristotle, 5, 22, 33, 154
Associationism, 52; and necessary judgments, 62ff.
Augustine, St., 22
Authority, 36
Avenarius, 53

Bache, 112
Bacon, Francis, 53
Bacon, Roger, 215
Bain, 114
Bakewell, 113
Baldwin, 47, 110
Balfour, 30, 35, 190
Balzer, 102
Bautain, 186
Bawden, 47
Bayle, 30
Bazaillais, 113
Beattie, 191
Beesly, 53
Belief, 11
Berkeley, 6, 60, 107
Bergson, intuitionism of, 39ff., 198
Boetzkes, 101
Bonnetty, 186

Boodin, 47
Bosanquet, 112, 122, 163, 172
Bowne, 113
Boutroux, 113
Bradley, 112, 114, 122, 130
Brentano, 155
Bridges, 53
Broad, 100, 118
Brunetière, 190
Brunschvicg, 112
Burnet, 30
Burtt, 216
Busse, 112

Caird, E., 112
Caird, J., 112
Calkins, 90, 113, 122
Caritoni, 113
Carneades, 30
Cassirer, 112
Causes of error, 207ff.
Certitude, 15; not a guarantee of truth, 16; spontaneous and philosophic, 20; evidence as ultimate motive of, 183
Charron, 30
Clarke, 216
Coffey, 20, 35, 59, 74, 85, 96, 101, 109, 115, 129, 136, 138, 145, 168, 172, 178, 179, 185
Cognition, definition of, 10
Cohen, 112
Coherence theory of truth, 172ff.
Comte, 53, 68
Concepts, origin of, 88; universality of, 90; validity of, 195ff.; and images, differences between, 57ff.
Conceptualism, 196ff.
Condillac, 53
Congreve, 53
Consciousness, 12

Correspondence theory of truth, 166ff.
Creighton, 113
Criterion of truth, 181ff.; in pragmatism, 187ff.; anti-intellectualistic, 190ff.
Critical dogmatism, 20
Critical realism, 160ff.; criticism of, 162ff.
Croce, 113

De Bonald, 186
Deduction, worth of, 203ff.
De Lammenais, 186, 187
Descartes, 6; method of, 24, 38, 68, 70, 112
De Vorges, 102
Dewey, 46
Dilthy, 112
Dogmatism, 19
Doubt, 15; universal methodic, 21
Drake, 100, 107, 116, 148, 160
Durkheim, 53

Eckhart, 39
Ego-centric predicament, 144
Emerson, 113
Empiricism, 52
Epistemology, definition of, 2; history of, 4; importance of, 4; nature of, 2; relation of to logic and psychology, 7; genesis of problem of, 16; data of, 23; method of, 24
Error, causes of, 207ff.
Eucken, 112
Euclid, 22
Evans, 160
Everett, 113
Evidence, as criterion of truth, 181ff.
Evolutionary theory of truth, 176ff.
Experience, 10.
Extramental world, perceptionist proof of, 102ff.; representationist proof of, 104ff.; knowledge of, 134ff.
Extreme realism, 92

Farges, 101
Fechner, 101
Ferrari, 53
Ferrier, 2
Fideism, 30, 186
Fouillée, 113
Fries, 191
Froebes, 102
Fullerton, 100, 107, 148, 150

Gardiner, 113
Gentile, 113
Geny, 101
Gorgias, 30
Gredt, 101
Green, 112, 122, 127
Gruender, 101, 102
Gunn, 43

Haldane, 113
Harris, 113
Harrison, 54
Hartmann, 100
Hegel, 121
Helmholtz, 68
Hibben, 112
Hicks, 100
Hobbes, 53
Hobhouse, 100
Hocking, 43, 113, 189
Hodgson, 112
Hoernlé, 110, 113, 122
Holt, 100, 157
Howison, 121
Huet, 30, 186
Humanism, 47
Hume, 6, 30, 53, 73
Husserl, 100, 155
Huxley, 53, 103

Idealism, subjective, 110ff.; objective, 111, 119ff.; cardinal principle of, 113; criticism of subjective, 114ff.; criticism of objective, 122ff.
Initial attitude toward knowledge, 14ff.
Innatism, 37
Instinct as criterion of truth, 190ff.
Instrumentalism, 46
Intellect, definition of, 12; and senses, distinction between, 86

INDEX

Intellectual knowledge not relative, 143
Intuitionism, 39ff.

Jacobi, 191
James, 44, 90, 155, 159, 174, 190, 197
Jeannière, 20, 35, 102, 136, 148, 185
Joachim, 172
Joad, 100, 109, 115, 126
John of the Cross, St., 39
Jouffroy, 30
Joyce, 74
Judgments, kinds of, 28; objectivity of, 93ff.; truth of, 202ff.

Kallen, 47
Kant, 6, 119; theory of knowledge of, 73ff.; criticism of theory of knowledge, 79ff.; moral dogmatism of, 191; conceptualism of, 196
Klein, 101
Knowledge, definition of, 9; origin of, 36ff.; of the extramental world, 134ff.; truth of, 195ff.
Krause, 112
Kremer, 160
Kuelpe, 100

Laas, 53
Lachelier, 112
Ladd, 113
Lahr, 102
Laird, 100, 107, 129
Leibniz, 37, 68, 70
Leighton, 49, 103
Lercher, 101
LeRoy, 43, 47, 113
Lewes, 53
Liebmann, 112
Lindsay, 43
Locke, 6, 112
Logic, relation of to epistemology, 7
Lossky, 73, 100, 107
Lotze, 112
Lovejoy, 100, 158

MacGregor, 115

Mach, 47, 112
MacIntosh, 115, 175
Mackintosh, 112
Maher, 59, 64, 114, 116, 118, 141, 144, 145
Mallock, 190
Martineau, 145
Marvin, 100
McGilvery, 100
McTaggart, 113, 121
Meinong, 100, 155
Mercier, 26, 67, 83, 102, 111, 112, 197, 201, 202
Michelitch, 101
Milhaud, 47
Mill, 57, 63, 203
Mivart, 59, 118
Moderate realism, exposition of, 86ff.; proof of truth of, 94ff.
Monistic idealism, criticism of, 131
Montague, 33, 49, 100, 157, 172, 177
Montaigne, 30, 33
Moore, 47
Moore, G. E., 100, 155, 175, 190
Moore, T. V., 59
Morselli, 53
Motive of certitude, evidence as, 183
Murray, 175

Natorp, 112
Nature of unperceived reality, 153
Nelson, 191
Neo-realism, 155ff.; criticism of, 158ff.
Newman, 215
Newton, 68
Noel, 101
Nominalism, 56ff.
Normal sense perception, conditions of, 140ff.
Nunn, 100

Objective idealism, 111, 119ff.
Objectivity of judgments, 93
Ontological truth, 167
Origin of concepts, 88ff.
Origin of knowledge, 36ff.

Ormond, 113
Oswald, 191

Papini, 47
Pascal, 30
Paulsen, 112
Peirce, 44
Perception, definition of, 56
Perceptionism, knowledge of extramental world according to, 100ff.; 135ff.; obections to, 147ff.
Perry, 100, 115, 125, 129, 145, 157
Pesch, 101
Phenomenalism, definition of, 134
Pitkin, 100
Plato, 5, 37, 92
Plotinus, 39
Poincaré, 47, 135
Positivism, exposition of, 53; criticism of, 56ff.
Pragmatism, origin of knowledge in, 44ff.; theory of truth in, 174ff.; criterion of truth in, 187ff.; relativism of, 176ff.; conceptualism of, 197ff.
Pratt, 100, 160, 175
Prichard, 9, 75, 85, 116, 197
Pringle-Pattison, 112, 126, 130
Protagoras, 30, 176
Psychology, relation of to epistemology, 7
Pyrrho, 5, 30

Rationalism, critical, 73ff.; pure, 70ff.
Realism, definition of, 99; proof of, 102; difficulties of, 151ff.
Reasoning, validity of deductive, 203ff.
Reflective thinking, 14
Reid, 100
Reid, Thomas, 191
Relations, in idealism, 126ff.; in realism, 129
Relativism, definition of, 176
Relativity of intellectual knowledge, 143
Relativity of sensation, 137ff.
Relativity theory of truth, 176ff.
Renouvier, 112

Representationism, 101; proof of extramental world in, 104; criticism of, 106
Ribot, 53
Rickaby, 168
Rickert, 112
Riehl, 53
Ritschl, 191
Rogers, 50, 100, 160, 172
Rosmini, 38
Royce, 49, 113, 122
Russell, 47
Russell, Bertrand, 43, 81, 100, 129, 148, 155

Sabatier, 112, 191
Sanchez, 30
Santayana, 100, 160
Schellwein, 101
Schiller, 47, 176, 197
Schleiermacher, 191
Schuppe, 112
Science, definition of, 11
Self-consciousness, meaning of, 12
Sellars, 100, 109, 160
Sensation, definition of, 56
Sensationalism, exposition of, 52ff.; criticism of, 56ff.; see Sensism
Senses, 55; trustworthiness of, 142; and intellect, distinction between, 86
Sense illusions, 151
Sense perception, conditions of normal and abnormal, 140ff.
Sense qualities, relativity of, 137ff.; subjectivity or objectivity of, 152
Sensism, history of, 53; criticism of, 56ff.; the basic axiom of, 66
Sentiment, feeling, will to believe, as criteria of truth, 190ff.
Sextus Empiricus, 5, 30
Sidgwick, 176
Simmel, 47
Skepticism, definition of, 29; examination of, 30
Smith, N. K., 73, 79
Socrates, 5
Solipsism in subjective idealism, 116

INDEX

Spaulding, 33, 69, 100, 115, 129, 145, 157, 173, 179, 190
Spencer, 53, 64, 107, 135
Spinoza, 70
Stephen, 43
Stewart, 43
Stewart, Dugald, 191
Stoeckel, 102
Stout, 62
Strong, 100, 160
Suprasensible beings, knowability of, 66ff.
Syllogism, positivistic objection to, 203ff.

Theresa, St., 39
Thilly, 85
Thinking, reflective, 14
Thomas, St., 9, 23, 88, 90, 91, 101, 129, 139, 141, 154, 167, 168, 177, 211
Traditionalism, 186
Trustworthiness of senses, 142
Truth, definition of, 167ff.; correspondence theory of, 166ff.; coherence theory of, 172ff.; pragmatic theory of, 174ff.; relativity of, 176ff.; *see also* Criterion of truth.
Truth of knowledge, 195ff.
Tufts, 47, 113
Turner, 158, 163

Tyndall, 53

Ultra-dogmatism, 19
Universal, relation of to individual, 199; *see* Concept
Utility, as truth, 174ff.; as a criterion of truth, 187ff.; *see* Pragmatic theory of truth

Vance, 4, 20, 35, 100, 102, 136, 148, 185
Ventura, 186
Verworen, 112

Walker, 20, 59, 107, 129, 133, 172, 174, 175, 185
Wallas, 216
Ward, 102, 121
Watson, 113
Weber, 76, 112
Wenley, 113
Whitehead, 100
Will to believe as substitute for intellect, 190ff.
William of Champeaux, 92
Windelband, 75, 112
Wolf, 100
Wolff, 70
Woodbridge, 100
Wundt, 68

Zeno, 32

DATE DUE